Mickey Tobin

THE ART
OF
POSITIVE PARENTING

Illustrations by Gay Kanuth

Published by
Greyden Press
Columbus, Ohio

Acknowledgments

To all of my family and extended family, I am grateful. Particularly, to my sons, David and Bruce, my daughters, Patty and Betsy, my grandchildren and in-law children and especially to Jim, my husband and best friend, thank you. Thank you for allowing me to use examples from our lives that helped demonstrate how much there is to learn.

And thank you to the T.A.P.P. teachers and Kathy Peterson who helped bring these ideas together.

And to Gigi Kegg and Dean Van Nest who helped make this project a reality.

THE ART
OF
POSITIVE PARENTING

Goals:

To build self-esteem in children by helping families provide a setting that allows children to become self-regulated and autonomous rather than parent regulated and dependent, in an atmosphere of love and acceptance where relationships depend upon a regard for feelings and mutual respect.

Mickey Tobin

CONTENTS

PREFACE

The Art of Positive Parenting (T.A.P.P.) is a six week (12 hour) class that promotes the role of the parent as the foundation of a healthy society.

The purpose of the T.A.P.P. project is to encourage effective parenting by promoting the value of parent education and by making it available, accessible and affordable.

I designed the T.A.P.P. program in 1978 and joined the staff of Crittenton Family Services in Columbus, Ohio in January of 1979. The T.A.P.P. program was a part of the family life education programs at that agency from 1979 until June 30, 1993. In 1980, the T.A.P.P. project received a small grant from the Acorn Fund of the Columbus Foundation to show that the T.A.P.P. material was viable and useful for a high risk population. From this demonstration project, T.A.P.P. developed a contract with Franklin County Children Services, our child protection agency. By 1992, T.A.P.P. was a six week (12 hour) component of every family life program at the Crittenton agency and successfully serving approximately 750 high risk clients referred from Franklin County Children Services each year. At the same time T.A.P.P. classes were made available to neighborhood parents who could pay a fee to take a class. Every effort was made to keep the fees affordable and the classes accessible. We offered a new series of classes every season in and around Columbus, Ohio.

The T.A.P.P. philosophy served as the bedrock of all family life program planning at Crittenton Family Services. The family life teachers received extensive training to teach The Art of Positive Parenting. Evaluations were uniformly excellent. A 1992 national evaluation from Family Service of America described T.A.P.P. as one of the best family life education programs in the country.

In 1993, my former supervisor, Kathy Peterson, and I formed a separate non-profit, education agency called T.A.P.P. - P L U S. Our purpose was to expand our reach and to continue to provide high quality parent education to a cross section of parents in Central Ohio.

OF POSITIVE PARENTING

The project is currently serving high risk parents referred from the courts as well as the parent populations from the following social service agencies: Alvis House, Traynor House, Volunteers of America Family Shelter, Parents Anonymous Groups, Access, Choices, House of Hope and Central Community House and clients of the Columbus Health Department and Maryhaven Inc. The suburban neighborhood classes also continue to flourish. At this time, we are serving approximately 1500 parents a year.

T.A.P.P. - P L U S has developed financial support from several resources. In 1994, T.A.P.P. received a renewable grant from Franklin County Children Services in conjunction with Central Community House, and a stabilization grant from the United Way of Columbus, Ohio. In 1995, T.A.P.P. received funding from The Columbus Foundation to serve parent populations from seven separate agencies, and from The Ingram - White Castle Foundation to serve parents referred from the Municipal Court System. The Columbus Health Department, Amethyst, Maryhaven, Bank One, Columbus Montessori, and A.T.&T. are also contracts that were committed to the 1995 class schedule. 1996 looks equally promising. We have collaborated with the Y.W.C.A. of Columbus, Ohio to launch a joint project that will eventually enable all parents to register in a T.A.P.P. class that fits their needs and their schedule. This project is titled "Teach the Parent, Reach the Child."

T.A.P.P. - P L U S also continues to offer a substantial number of neighborhood classes where individual client fees provide a portion of the cost and community funds support the remaining cost. The neighborhood classes are offered in churches, schools and community centers or any place where parents gather together to request a class. T.A.P.P. classes can be adapted to fit the specific needs of different populations. At Bank One for example, twelve one hour sessions offered at noon are more suitable than six two hour sessions offered in the evening.

Partners for Positive Parenting, a volunteer membership support group formed in August 1993, helps provide scholarship money for those individuals who call the office to take a neighborhood class but are unable to pay a full fee.

The T.A.P.P. training plan is unique and successful and has enabled me to train other parents to teach and share this valuable material. Therefore, T.A.P.P. classes are reaching many more parents than I would have been able to teach by myself. Because T.A.P.P. has been in existence for so many years, T.A.P.P. - P L U S now receives many inquiries from friends and relatives of parents who have enjoyed the benefits of using the T.A.P.P. skills, asking if the principles of T.A.P.P. are available in book form. While there is no substitute for taking a class, (parents benefit so much from learning with other parents and from other parents), it is not always possible for parents to do so, especially parents who live in other places and are unable to find high quality parent education.

For many years T.A.P.P. graduates have also asked for a book. They want a convenient reminder to reinforce what they have learned in class. The help I have been able to offer so far is in two volumes of tips (see bibliography) that are designed to help parents and children through difficult times. Until last June 30th, when I officially retired, I was unable to find the time to organize the class material and the tips into a book for T.A.P.P. parents, their friends and families. This year, thanks to the help and support of many people, I have been encouraged to do so.

I am indebted to the bibliography and have tried to credit all sources that have contributed to this material. The biggest difference between T.A.P.P. and other available parent education programs is my determination to eliminate roadblocks as a preliminary necessity before communication and problem solving skills can be effective. Students of parent education programs will also notice that I do not recommend family meetings. I am reluctant to advise such meetings because I think they are a temptation for parents to once again slip into a patriarchal role, and I think family problems are best resolved by the persons who own the problem without involving other family members. However,

OF POSITIVE PARENTING

family meetings might be helpful to encourage participation in decision making concerning family work and family fun.

The skills outlined in Chapter Four include some guidelines for setting limits that are unique to T.A.P.P. as are the description and definition of rules in the same section. Many of the exercises, all of the tips, and most of the teaching dialogues are unique to T.A.P.P. and when adapted from other sources, the sources are credited immediately in the text.

Long experience answering parents' questions and concerns about child rearing, has given me insights to specific family problems that can help a parent and a child through difficult times. I have learned as much from the parents I have taught as they have learned from T.A.P.P. Almost all of the examples in this book are stories of the successes and failures that have been reported in class. My own four children deserve credit for motivation. Many times during the twenty to thirty years that they were in our house, I felt (as Faber & Mazlish have said) "There has to be a better way!"

I am also indebted to the T.A.P.P. teachers, present and past, (in 17 years, I have trained approximately 35 teachers) and especially to Kathy Peterson who believed in the curriculum so completely that I was able to do things I would never have thought possible.

T.A.P.P. currently has 16 active teachers working and teaching for T.A.P.P. - P L U S. Only two of these teachers are full time employees. The rest are part time. Many of them work at other occupations during the day and teach classes at night. All of the teachers are parents who have taken the class and found the material particularly helpful and important. One teacher has been with me for 14 years and three others for over 10 years. Six of the teachers are African American. Many of our African American clients are more comfortable learning about child rearing from fellow African Americans. We meet as a staff once a month and share the things we have learned about interpreting the T.A.P.P. concepts so that they are believable, well-received and understood. I know of no other parent education program that has been this successful in reaching parents from all backgrounds and receiving broad based community financial support to do so.

The book is divided into six chapters. Each chapter is designed to be read in sequence with time in between to practice the skills as they are introduced. The sections entitled Practice Makes Progress reintroduce and reaffirm the skills, providing additional learning opportunities for the reader. Enjoy!

It's never too late.

No matter how old your children are,
your relationships will be enhanced
every time you are able to use
a positive parenting skill.

Why Parent Training?

WHY?

When we stopped beating children with a board or a belt, no-one....no-one ....stepped in to help us learn a more positive form of discipline. We learned instead to yell, to scream, to lecture, judge, scold and label.

We learned to use shame and embarrassment as a form of discipline in the classroom and at home. We thought this conduct was appropriate and necessary in order to socialize children and to teach them the difference between right and wrong.

But today we realize that this style of child rearing is damaging and ineffective. It makes children feel fearful and full of revenge. It destroys self-esteem, causes bad feelings, starts arguments and leads to loss of control....and besides, it proves ineffective in re-directing unacceptable behavior. Today, successful methods of discipline depend upon respect.

Traditionally, the family was patriarchal. Family members relied upon the father for authority and discipline. Wives responded to the dictates of their husbands and children obeyed the orders of their parents. Parents were not concerned with self-esteem. They were concerned with feeding us, housing us and educating us, but not with how we felt about ourselves.

Today, the family is more democratic. Wives have an equal voice in the order of the household, and children are more cooperative when they are involved in the decision making process. Children respond to respect and learn from parents to respect in return. Family discipline and order depend, not upon the authority of the parents, but upon mutual respect and regard for the feelings and rights of self and others.

OF POSITIVE PARENTING

Statistics tell us that children are rejecting families that deny them an atmosphere of mutual respect. Children cannot get divorces. They are forced to separate by running away, by over using drugs, through delinquent behavior that results in legal separation, through teen-age pregnancy and even through suicide. Statistics also tell us that the primary cause of such behaviors is low self-esteem.

So today, there is no choice. Unlike our parents, we must be concerned with self-esteem. We need to learn parenting skills based on mutual respect. We need to recognize the importance of feelings. We need to learn how to build self-esteem and encourage responsibility. We need to help children become self-regulated and autonomous rather than parent-regulated and dependent. We need to learn the art of parenting positively.

Troubled parents, caught with an outdated and ineffective style of child rearing learned from their parents, need a systematic program of high quality parent education. Positive parenting is an art to be learned. The Art of Positive Parenting skills outlined in this book are dedicated to this end. They are designed to help parents and children live in an atmosphere of mutual respect.

Most parents want more happiness for their children than they feel for themselves. The intentions of most parents are of the highest order. Their performance, however, suffers from lack of information and lack of training for the job.

This book is designed to help provide that training. It is divided into six chapters. I recommend parents read and work each chapter separately and in sequence, allowing time in between to practice and apply what you have learned.

The bibliography is important. I have borrowed concepts freely and tried to incorporate them into an orderly presentation of skills. I have credited each contribution as it is used. I would urge readers to pursue further study from any of the resources listed in the bibliography.

I especially recommend what I call "the wonderful words of Haim Ginott". Most of them have been preserved for us through the fine work of Adele Faber and Elaine Mazlish.

WHERE ARE WE GOING?

We were all perfect parents until we had children. And then the problems and pitfalls of parenting were upon us before we had a chance to think through how effective our practices were in terms of what we wanted our children to experience. It's never too late. No matter how old your children are, your relationships will be enhanced every time you are able to use a positive parenting skill. Ask yourself, "What are my goals?", "What do I want for my children?" and "What do I want for myself?"

I have designed the following goal for all parents, but you may want to design your own goal, in your own words, for your own child.

I believe most of us want our children to live and to grow----to feel good about themselves, to have high self-esteem----to be self-regulated, to be able to take care of themselves---and to have a high regard for the feelings and rights of others.

I believe families want to live in an atmosphere of mutual respect.

Establishing goals will help you chart a course of action and give you something to measure against. It will also help you answer the following questions.

Are the interactions I am having with my child leading toward or away from my goals?

Is my relationship with my child being strengthened or weakened through the words I use?

Do I need to "unlearn" a lifetime of damaging talk and replace it with responses that build self-esteem?

Most of us use the style of child-rearing that our parents used. Not all of their practices were damaging. List for yourself your feelings and thoughts about how you were parented.

Write down your answers to the following questions.

What am I doing that works.....that makes me feel good....that reaches my goal?

_____

_____

_____

_____

Did my parents do these things?
Yes_____No_____

What am I doing that doesn't work.....that makes me feel bad.....that leads away from my goal?

_____

_____

_____

_____

Did my parents do this too?
Yes_____No_____

Did it work for them?
Yes_____No_____

How did it make me feel when I was a child?

_____

_____

_____

_____

Can I learn some new skills.....can I change......can I unlearn a lifetime of damaging talk and replace it with responses that build self-esteem and mutual respect?

Yes!

HOW DO WE STOP COMMUNICATION? HOW DO WE MAKE CHILDREN FEEL?

To be successful positive parents, we need to understand the importance of feelings, the two-fold nature of feelings and to identify and erase the habitual parent responses that stop communication and deny feelings.

We call these responses roadblocks, a useful term introduced to me by Thomas Gordon in the book *Parent Effectiveness Training.*

In this section, you will be learning the single most important thing parents need to learn to improve their parenting skills:

Stop Using Roadblocks!

What are the roadblocks?
How do they sound?
How do they make children feel?

Some roadblocks are obviously damaging.

1. We criticize!
2. We threaten!

OF POSITIVE PARENTING

We learned instead to yell, to scream, to lecture, judge, scold and label. This makes children feel fearful and full of revenge.

3. We blame and compare!
4. We shame and embarrass!
5. We name call and label!
6. We lecture and preach!
7. We order, direct and command!

Other roadblocks might seem less damaging but also raise doubts, create anxiety, deny feelings and stop communication.

1. We reassure.
2. We sympathize.
3. We divert.
4. We question.
5. We offer unbelievable, "global" praise, and
6. We are too quick to suggest solutions to problems.

Roadblocks are phrases that damage the relationship between parents and children. Roadblocks convey a message of disrespect. Respect needs a two way street. If you want respect from your child, he must feel respect from you. Parents who use roadblocks with children show little or no respect for their child.

Roadblocks stop communication. Roadblocks hurt children and damage self-esteem. Roadblocks deny the existence of feelings.

Some roadblocks are overtly disrespectful. Recognize how they feel to children.

1. Criticizing - "You're so clumsy!"
2. Threatening - "If I catch you doing that again I'll....."
3. Blaming and comparing - "Your sister didn't have any trouble....."
4. Shaming and embarrassing - "Shame on you...."

5. Name calling and labeling - "You're such a picky eater!"
6. Lecturing and preaching, moralizing - "A penny saved is a penny ..."
7. Ordering, directing and commanding - "Stop crying right now!"

Other roadblocks are covert or hidden. They are not as obviously harmful but do raise doubts, create anxiety, deny respect and also hurt self-esteem.

1. Reassuring - "Well I think you're beautiful!"
2. Sympathizing - "You poor thing..."
3. Diverting - "It's not important...have an apple...a cookie."
4. Questioning - probing. " Did you ask them nicely?"
5. "Global" praising - "You're wonderful...."
6. Suggesting solutions. "Why don't you play with your sister..."

Throughout this book, I will try to demonstrate through sample conversations (teaching dialogues) the damage that roadblocks create and that even reassurance, sympathy, questioning, diversion and praise can cause bad feelings and low self-esteem. The teaching dialogues allow parents to hear how roadblocks sound in conversations, and to feel how they hurt children and stop communication.

THE IMPORTANCE OF FEELINGS

Feelings are....they exist...they are real. Some feelings feel good--comfortable--constructive--helpful. Some feelings feel bad--uncomfortable--angry--hurtful.

Good feelings thrive on acceptance, listening and love.

Bad feelings thrive on judgments, the roadblocks, because they stop or block good feelings and promote or increase bad feelings and low self-esteem.

Faber & Mazlish in their book *How to Talk So Kids Will Listen* explore the direct connection between how children feel and how they behave. "When kids feel right, they'll behave right. How do we help them to feel right? By accepting their feelings!"

The problem is parents don't usually accept children's feelings. They "roadblock" them instead...So once again, reflect on the importance of this first skill.

Before introducing the first teaching dialogue, let's explore the two-fold nature of feelings - good feelings and bad feelings. (Remember, there is a direct connection between how children feel and how they behave.) Good feelings are better to have than bad feelings. Parents want their children to have good feelings. But most of us don't realize that until bad, angry feelings are out in the open, until they are heard and accepted, they will not go away. When we listen without roadblocks to bad, angry feelings, they begin to dissolve. **When bad feelings are accepted without judgment, good feelings take their place.**

What about good feelings? Can we learn to nurture our own good feelings so that we can help our children develop good feelings?

Most of us are unable to tell good things about ourselves. We were told it was "conceited". We were told it was bad manners. We were told not to brag.... And we learned not to tell good things. Eventually, we were unable to think of a good thing, let alone able to tell a friend something good that we had done.

Now we know that self-esteem needs nourishment from everyone ..... especially from ourselves. So think of a good thing that you have done today or last week or last year.....A big thing or a little thing, it doesn't matter, but something that made you feel good about yourself.

Feel this good feeling inside yourself. If you can, share this good thing with a friend. Share your good thoughts with your family too. Your children will learn from you that feeling good about yourself is permissible and important.

To explore bad feelings, think of a time in your life when you were very, very angry. You may have been a child or it may have been recently. Try to recall it vividly in your mind. Remember small details. Think about the feelings you had before the anger. Thomas Gordon in *Parent Effectiveness Training* explains that anger is a secondary feeling and in my experience it usually is preceded by other bad feelings. You might have first felt frustration, fright or embarrassment. Make a list of the bad feelings you had before the anger.

Good feelings are nicer to have than bad feelings. Adele Faber & Elaine Mazlish in Chapter II of *Liberated Parents, Liberated Children* state, "until angry, hurtful feelings are out in the open, until they are heard and accepted, they do not change. Good feelings cannot flow in until the bad ones have emptied out."

In summary, so far we have established the following crucial connections: roadblocks cause bad feelings; children that are full of bad feelings tend to behave in unacceptable ways; children that are full of good feelings tend to behave in acceptable ways; bad feelings thrive on roadblocks; good feelings thrive on listening, acceptance and love.

TEACHING DIALOGUES

In order to understand and change our style of child-rearing and stop using roadblocks - we need to examine them.

How do they sound in conversation?

How do they make children feel?

How do they stop communication?
How do they hurt self esteem and mutual respect?

The first teaching dialogue is a conversation that has been used for many years in the T.A.P.P. classes. As you read this conversation, try to be Patty, that is to feel what Patty feels as Mother uses one roadblock after another until the conversation disintegrates and the relationship wears thin. Patty is about five years old. Mother is well-intentioned but unskilled in giving positive responses.

Patty:
Billy and Peggy won't let me jump rope with them and I don't have anybody to play with.
Mother:
Did you ask them nicely? (Questioning - Blaming)
Patty:
They said, "tick-tock the game is locked" and you know what that means.
Mother:
I never heard that before. Do you know any other rhymes like that? (Diverting)
Patty:
No I don't, and I sure don't think they're being very fair!
Mother:
Well it sounds like you're not in a very good mood to play. You'd better put on a smile. (Criticizing - Blaming)
Patty:
I don't feel like smiling, and I'm not going to invite them to my party either!
Mother:
Why don't you play with your sister. She'd love to hear some records. (Suggesting solutions)
Patty:
I don't want to play with records - and who wants to

play with a baby?

This dialogue probably ends up with Patty being sent to her room. At the very least, the conversation has turned into a non-productive argument that leads away from your goals. The roadblocks are interfering and controlling. Can you feel how they make Patty feel?

List at least three feelings Patty is experiencing in this conversation.

_____

_____

_____

Before you read the corrected dialogue, understand that there are many successful ways to respond to a child who is full of bad feelings. In Chapter Two we will learn more about responses that are not interfering and controlling, responses that will successfully replace the familiar roadblocks. In the following corrected teaching dialogue, listen for three important things.

1. Listen for the silences. What the Mother doesn't say is as significant as what she does say. Her pauses give Patty a chance to generate her own ideas. They also give Mother a chance to frame an appropriate response. (The pause is reflected by a series of dots. e.g. ......)

2. Listen to Mother repeat back or re-state what Patty has said.

3. Listen for the a-ha line, when Patty begins to solve her own problem.

Restate what your child has said to you: "Betsy can't play the way you want to play."

Patty:
Billy and Peggy won't let me jump rope with them, and I don't have anybody to play with.
Mother:
Oh?...... (with sympathy, tries to think about how Patty is feeling.).......You'd really like to play with somebody!
Patty:
I wish I had a sister who could jump rope.
Mother:
Hmmm.......Betsy can't play the way you want to play.
Patty:
You can't jump rope if you can hardly walk or talk.
Mother:
(Nodding) ......She's too young to jump rope!
Patty:
She can't play jump rope games but we play music games. (The a-ha !)
Mother:
You like to play music with Betsy?
Patty:
Yes, she loves it if I play a record and we dance too!
Mother:
Sounds like fun!
Patty:
I guess I'll play our new one, is that okay with you?
Mother:
Sure is!

This Mother not only helps Patty feel better, she also feels better about herself and her performance as a parent. Patty and Mother are still friends and feel respect for each other. The Mother's words have not been interfering and controlling. The Mother's attitude has conveyed faith that Patty can work out her own solution.

THE "GOOD MOTHER' SYNDROME

Most parents, confronted with a situation where a child is experiencing a problem, respond the same way their own parents did, and because we have not had a chance to learn a better way, we keep making the same mistakes our parents made. Like them, we often play the role of what we believe is a "good mother". "Good mother" is a generic term. The "good mother" can be male or female. As a matter of fact, I have known many fathers who were expert "good mothers". I am reminded of one in particular who chose where his son would attend college, escorted his son to the school and stayed with him during registration week, spoke personally with each of the boy's professors and requested that they inform him regularly about the boy's progress. Desperate to establish his independence from his family, the boy dropped out of school halfway through the second semester and ran away to marry a sixteen year old girl from the town.

The "good mother" lives her child's life for him. She's over involved, too talkative, chief advisor, director and implementor. She knows how her children should act, look, talk, study and play. She tries to choose their clothes and their friends. Her own sense of self is directly related to her child's successes and failures. She is overprotective and controlling. She is also unappreciated, frustrated and exhausted.

The "good mother" uses roadblocks to orchestrate her job. She pleads, begs, blames, shames, criticizes and threatens. She lectures and preaches but is rarely heard. She is adept at suggesting solutions to problems that belong to her child. She does not listen to and respect her child's point of view.

Her child grows up feeling diminished and incapable. He also feels resentful and angry. The "good mother" has conveyed to him through her roadblocks that he is acceptable only if he does things her way! He has lost the opportunity to build self-esteem. He has no sense of participation in decision making. He has not been allowed to contribute, to make choices and to feel the satisfaction of accepting responsibility for himself. The roadblocks have robbed him of two crucial feelings that are at the core of self-esteem in children. One - feeling loved and accepted, and two - feeling capable and worthwhile.

If your parents lectured, you probably lecture in the name of the "good mother".

If your parents shamed and blamed, you probably do the same, in the name of the "good mother".

Roadblocks are the parents' way of controlling their children's lives.

Instead of controlling, we can learn to help our children become separate, independent people who feel lovable and capable by giving up roadblocks and learning to listen instead.

The following exercise is adapted from Thomas Gordon's second book, *PET in Action.*

A fourteen year old boy tells his parent about a problem he is having in school. The parent responds in several different ways.

Boy:
"I hate my teacher and I hate school! She doesn't teach us anything It's boring!"

Parent:
1. "Now you don't mean that!"

2. "She's doing the best she can!"

3. "You're talking like a spoiled child!"

4. "If you don't pay more attention, you'll fail!"

5. "But honey, she's a lovely person!"

6. "You don't like your teacher and you hate school !"

How many of the responses are road-blocks?_____

Which responses increase the boy's bad feelings?_____

Which responses deny feelings and stop communication?_____

Which response will encourage the boy to keep talking?_____

Many roadblocks start with familiar phrases that can give us a clue that we are on the wrong track. If you hear yourself saying, "Don't you think you oughta..." or "Why don't you...", you will have a clue that you are trying to control your child to conform to what you believe is the best course of action for him. You may indeed know a better way. You may not know a better way. You have the privilege of choosing for yourself but parental rights do not give you the privilege of choosing for your child. The important lesson is that he learn to solve his own problems, to make his own decisions and to feel the satisfaction of accepting responsibility for himself. Don't worry, there will be time to share your thoughts and experiences because your listening responses will improve your relationship and your child will be more likely to hear what you have to contribute.

Concentrate on how roadblocks make children feel. It will help you unlearn the lifetime of damaging talk and replace it with responses that build self-esteem and mutual respect.

Back to Patty for a moment. Patty felt left out of the game. Most of us have experienced this bad feeling. Mother's response, "Did you ask them nicely?" made Patty feel blamed. She felt that Mother thought it was her fault. She then felt defensive, argumentative, like a failure, misunderstood, and finally, very angry!

Parents miss many opportunities to help children handle their feelings and to build a good relationship when they rely on these kinds of responses. Every parent-child interaction is an opportunity. Don't let your interactions with your child be missed opportunities that send the wrong message and damage self-esteem.

In Chapter Two, we will talk more about responses parents can use that will build better relationships. They require an attitude of acceptance. Dorothy Briggs in her book *Your Child's Self-Esteem* calls it trust. Trust that your child can work things out and let him. Your attitude is the key.

Review the exercises and suggestions outlined in this section before you move on to the next chapter of this book. I also recommend that you let some time go by to practice this first and most important skill before you read Chapter Two. For the next three or four days, pause before you respond to a child full of bad feelings. Then, answer with an empathic silence or a one word response such as "Hmm", or "Really". Concentrate on unlearning a lifetime of damaging talk. **Stop using roadblocks!**

Again, I firmly believe that eliminating roadblocks is the most important single thing parents can do to improve their parenting skills. The skills outlined in the rest of this book, the listening, the language of description, limit - choice - action, high expectations, natural consequences, problem solving and, most of all, modeling will not be effective in families where parents are still using roadblocks.

Practice Makes Progress

If your parents did not listen to your bad feelings, remember that most adults are reluctant to listen to children's unhappy feelings. In fact, they usually try to talk them out of feeling bad. "Don't cry! Have a cookie, some milk, an apple. Please feel better soon!" Today we know that bad feelings grow stronger when they are bottled up and not heard. It is only when we can talk about bad feelings that good feelings can come in to take their place. The expression of anger allows room for joy---the expression of jealousy, room for love---embarrassment, room for pride.

Because we want our children to have happy memories of childhood, we must learn to listen to their feelings without approval or disapproval, without praise or criticism. Beware of spoiling your efforts by adding a roadblock. There is no better way to insure the failure of a parent's listening than adding on a roadblock. When parents first learn to listen to children's feelings, "You're worried about school ", It's no fun to play alone" , it is very tempting to add, "Why don't you study more?" - "Did you ask them nicely?" This will destroy the benefits of listening to feelings, and rob your children of the opportunity to solve their own problems.

In Chapter One, we have talked about roadblocks. All of us use roadblocks to control the actions of other people and unfortunately, many parents are caught with a style of child rearing learned from their parents, a style laced with roadblocks that deny feelings and deny respect. A style that says, "Clean up your room" - "Do the dishes" -

"Stop crying" - "Big boys don't cry!" - "You're so spoiled" - "Comb your hair" - "You're stupid" - "You're clumsy" - "Tuck your shirt in" - "Why do you hate that dress, it looks great on you"....all phrases that hurt children, deny feelings and chip away at self-esteem.

The following exercise will help you experience how roadblocks make people feel. It is adapted from *How To Talk So Kids Will Listen* by Adele Faber and Elaine Mazlish.

Imagine you're at work as a waitress at a restaurant. Your employer (also the cook) asks you to do an extra job for him - tabulating the previous days receipts. He wants it ready by the end of the day. You mean to take care of it immediately, but because of a series of emergencies that come up, you completely forget. Things are so hectic, you barely have time for your own lunch.

As you and the rest of the day shift workers are getting ready to go home, your boss comes over to you and asks for the finished tabulation. Quickly you try to explain how unusually busy you were today.

He interrupts you. In a loud, angry voice he shouts, "I'm not interested in your excuses! What the hell do you think I'm paying you for -- to sit around all day on your butt? " As you open your mouth to speak, he says, "Save it," and stalks back to the kitchen.

Your co-workers pretend not to have heard. You finish gathering your things and leave the restaurant. On the way home you meet a friend. You're still so upset that you find yourself telling your friend what had just taken place.

Your friend tries to help you in several different ways. As you read each response, tune in to your immediate feeling reaction! Circle either *Good* or *Not Good*.

You say to your friend:
" So anyway, that's what happened and I don't know what to do!"

His responses:
1. "Oh come on - forget it - how about a cup of coffee!"
   How does this feel?   *Good*   *Not Good*

2. "You poor thing...that's terrible...I'm so sorry for you!"
   How does this feel?   *Good*   *Not Good*

3. "That was pretty stupid! You need to pay more attention to him, after all, he's the boss."
   How does this feel?   *Good*   *Not Good*

4. "Look life is like that! Things don't always turn out the
   way we want. You have to learn to take things in stride."
   How does this feel?   *Good*   *Not Good*

5. "You know what I think you should do? Tomorrow
   morning go straight to your boss - say ' Look I was
   wrong.' Then sit right down and finish that work. If
   you're smart you won't get trapped like that again!"
   How does this feel?   *Good*   *Not Good*

6. "Didn't you realize he'd be angry? Didn't you know
   he'd do that? Why didn't you try to explain?"
   How does this feel?   *Good*   *Not Good*

7. "Mmmm - that sounds rough! How embarrassing ---
   in front of all those people!"
   How does this feel?   *Good*   *Not Good*

Whether the problem is solved or not,
the listening skills are successful
when the lines of communication remain open
and the interaction feels constructive.

When The Child Owns The Problem

LISTENING - THE UNIVERSAL SKILL

If we are to understand our children - their feelings and behavior - then we must sharpen the memories from our own childhood.

The purpose of this exercise is to remind us of our own childhood feelings and experiences so that we can remember how important feelings are to children...Remember, children feel what they feel!

Imagine you are in a conversation with an older, good friend, a kind and considerate person who does not give evaluations, judgments and advice.

Use the following sentence fragments to begin your memory journey. Try to remember specific situations that are triggered by the sentence fragment. No matter what you say, your friend will not use roadblocks but will listen instead.

> As a child I remember a holiday that
> was........
> My sister and I were always........
> My Mother thought I was.........
> The teacher that I liked best was a person
> who.........
> When I was a little girl I wanted to grow
> up to be a ....
> My parents were very...........
> Our favorite family vacation was ....
> I felt very happy when..........
> When I was 10 years old, my best friend
> was...........

Were your childhood memories happy or sad? Can you remember times when you felt sad or discouraged? Can you remember times when you felt happy and important? When you were a child, did anyone listen to your bad feelings? Did anyone care about your good feelings?

From this experience:
I learned that I...
I was surprised that I...
I was saddened that I...
I never knew....
I enjoyed...

Childhood memories tell us that some roadblocks are far worse than others. We have also learned that giving up roadblocks and listening to feelings is a universal skill. In other words, this is a skill that can be useful and positive in all areas of your life. Your response can make a difference when *anyone* in your life is feeling bad. Bad feelings empty out and good feelings take their place when *all* people are heard and understood.

Whether it's your parent, your child, your boss or your spouse, learn to listen to the other person's problem. Accept the way he feels. Give the feeling a name - and resist adding on reassurances, suggestions, questions or advice.

Reassurances are not believable. Diversions are ignored. Suggestions get rejected. Lectures fall on deaf ears. And people who feel bad, feel worse when they are questioned, probed and analyzed.

Universally, bad feelings empty out and good feelings take their place when people's bad feelings are heard and understood.

Following are three teaching dialogues that demonstrate this point. The first is adapted from Dr. Haim Ginott's *Between Parent & Teenager.*

Instead of:

David:
I didn't get the job!
Dad:
Your application was too late! I told you to send it in last week.
David:
It was not - the deadline was Monday - I dropped it off on Monday.
Dad:
And look at you - you could have had your hair cut, and worn a coat and tie.
David:
People don't dress like that today, besides - you always think it's my fault. You always blame me.
Dad:
You'd better pay attention to how you look before your next interview!
David:
What interview - I'm not gonna try for any more jobs - I'll never get hired anyway. I'm not good enough. It's just no use!

A listening response:
David, "I didn't get the job."
Dad, "Hmm. You really wanted that job."

Try some listening responses:

David:
I didn't get the job!
Dad:
Mmm - You really wanted that job, didn't you.
David:
I sure did. I know I could do the work!
Dad:
You were qualified all right.

David:

Yeah - a lot of good that did me!

Dad:

You thought your job problems would be over.

David:

Well I guess it's not the end of the world. I've got two more interviews - maybe I'll get lucky. I think I'll wear a coat *and* tie next time.

This Dad listened without approval or disapproval - without praise or criticism.

The next teaching dialogue is an example from the workplace. It is a conversation between a supervisor and a parent educator, adapted from a very real conversation between me and one of our T.A.P.P. parenting instructors.

Instructor:

You put too many people in that class last night. Eighteen is too many - we were hot and crowded and there weren't enough chairs.

Supervisor:

Why didn't you turn the heat down? And I'm sure there are some folding chairs in the storage room.

Instructor:

Why did you let it get so big? People feel cheated. There isn't enough time for everyone.

Supervisor:

I never know how many will show up -- and besides, three women brought their husbands without telling me. You'll do fine--you can handle it.

Instructor:

I think you should tell those three they can't attend-- there isn't room!

The work place is a *wise* place to practice good
listening responses. In the following corrected dialogue,
notice that if you listen effectively two or three times, the
other person can begin to tolerate some suggestions without stopping open communication.

Listening Responses:

Instructor:
You put too many people in that class last night--eigh-
teen is too many!
Supervisor:
Mmm, you're right--eighteen is a big class.
Instructor:
We were hot and crowded and there weren't enough chairs!
Supervisor:
Eighteen is too many!
Instructor:
And the people feel cheated--there isn't enough time for
everyone to participate.
Supervisor:
That room would be crowded with twelve.
Instructor:
Well--I did get through the material--they loved it--and
I think they'll all be back.
Supervisor:
Should I try to find another teacher?--and break into two
sessions?
Instructor:
Nooo-not this time--but try not to take so many names
in the spring.
Supervisor:
I sure will -- thanks Marie.

The following is also a true story. It demonstrates
again that listening is a universal skill. It also demon-

strates that even well intentioned reassurances are not effective because they roadblock people's feelings.

My friend Kathy is taking complete responsibility for the care of her elderly mother, Katie. Katie's mind moves in and out of reality and she needs full time, around the clock, nursing care. This is provided in Kathy's home.

Last fall Kathy's home had a kitchen fire. The smoke damage was extensive. After the repairs were completed, the insurance company recommended de-fogging the entire house every few months for a year. Katie and her nurse could not stay in the house during this time. Kathy arranged for them to stay in the nurse's home instead.

Katie was very fearful of this new experience. She trembled, she clung to Kathy and she began to slip out of touch with reality.

The nurses responses were familiar reassurances, but they did not help.

Nurse:
Don't worry Sweetie!...It'll be all right! We're gonna have a fine time together! You'll see. Please don't be afraid.

Katie continued to tremble and started to cry. Kathy's listening responses were soothing, calming and helpful!

Kathy:
We've never been here before!......This is really scary!......
Katie:
You've got that right!
Kathy:
Let's just sit here and hold hands until we feel safe!

Katie stopped trembling and soon let go of Kathy's hand. Kathy was able to leave for work because her mother felt calm thanks to Kathy's listening skills.

Reassurances are not believable......listening to feelings helps!

It's hard work to have to listen to a person's emotional out pouring. It's difficult to resist asking questions or giving advice. It takes practice and concentration! We need to look into and beyond what a person says. We need to identify what he feels. We need to keep our goal in mind, and to remember that roadblocks start arguments and hurt people.

The skill involved is **Listen to Feelings.** As we have pointed out in Chapter One, there are many ways to listen effectively. Don't feel that you need to memorize a formula, or name out loud each feeling the child is experiencing. Some guidelines for successful listening are:

31

Listen to feelings: "We've never been here before -- this is really scary!"

> Listen with full attention.
> Restate, in your own words, what the person
>   has just said to you.
> Use empathic silence. (You do not need to
>   verbalize this skill. Pause and give yourself
>   a minute to silently identify how your child
>   is feeling.)
> Give the feeling a name. "You're angry!"
> Respond with a word..."Hmmm", "Wow!"

In *How To Talk So Kids Will Listen,* Faber & Mazlish suggest two additional listening techniques that can be effective.

The first additional suggestion is, sometimes, not always, you can join the child's feelings in fantasy. Start this with "You wish". The parents in our classes report that they find this especially successful with young children.

> "You really wish you had a big drink of cold
> water right now!"
> "You wish we could buy every toy truck
> in the store!"

The second, is write it down. The child will know his feelings are recognized when you take out a paper and pen and write down what he has asked for. Again this is especially helpful with young children.

> "I know you'd like those new crayons, I'm
> going to write that down right now!"

Now you are ready to write your own corrected dialogue. This can be great practice for the real world. I will provide the roadblocking dialogue, you can choose the appropriate responses for the corrected dialogue.

Try to demonstrate the availability of many choices for a correct response.   You can restate (re-word) what the child has said,   pause and use empathic silence, respond with one word, give the feeling a name, start with "You wish", or write it down. There are lots of good ways to respond to a person filled with bad feelings. Practice using all of them.   The following dialogue is between a mother and her fifteen year old son.

Joey:
"I'm going to drop history."
Mom:
"What do you mean you're going to drop history---you can't do that---you'll need it to graduate!"
Joey:
"The teacher isn't fair, she gives too much work--I can't do it all!"
Mom:
"What you need is a study plan -- and less television! You're sister didn't have any trouble in that class!"

Joey:
"You think it's my fault -- you always
blame me!"
Mom:
"I'm not listening to any more of this --
your father'll speak to you about history
when he gets home!"
Joey:
"He won't speak to me tonight because
I'm leaving!"

Now practice several successful listening responses to Joey.

Joey:
"I'm gonna drop history."

33

*Give the feeling a
name: "You're worried
about history."*

_____

_____

_____

_____

_____

_____

_____

_____

_____

_____

_____

QUALITY TIME &
CONSTRUCTIVE INTERACTIONS

In Dr. Haim Ginott's second book, *Between Parent
& Child*, he reminds us of the parental obligation to deal

constructively with accidental mishaps. Betty, age six, spilled milk all over the table during breakfast. She looked fearfully at her mother.

Betty:
Ahh -- I'm so stupid!

Mother:
That's not what happens when the milk spills.
Betty:
What happens?
Mother:
We say, "the milk spilled, hand me a sponge to clean it up."
Betty:
That's all? Hand me a sponge?
Mother:
That's all -- and here's the sponge.
Betty:
Thanks Mom!

When the milk spills -- hand them a sponge.

Betty will long remember this wise lesson. Deal constructively with accidental mishaps. How much would she have learned from criticism? "Now look at what you've done! Can't you be more careful? You always spill your milk! Don't be in such a hurry!"

Remember every parent child interaction is an opportunity to build a good relationship based on mutual respect. It is the quality of the interaction that matters the most. Today's parents need to worry not only about the amount of time they are able to spend but also about the quality of the time they spend. Dealing with mishaps constructively contributes to quality time.

Much has been written about quality time. Quality time implies that time together must enhance the relationship, build self esteem, respect, affection and acceptance. It obligates the parent to construct time that will build good memories for both parent and child. Parents struggle to make time together free from conflict and full of pleasant happenings, a tall order! Beware, this can lead to permissive parenting that caves in to whims and wants.

Self esteem, respect and acceptance come from contributing rather than receiving----from giving, not taking----from performing a task instead of being entertained. Parents and children who talk to one another while working together can be spending quality time. Learning together is also an opportunity for quality time. The secret is in sharing the work, sharing the result, sharing the learning and through using the listening skills instead of the more familiar roadblocks to orchestrate time together that is quality time.

In constructive interactions that provide quality time, it is also important for the parent to model self-love and self-respect. Respect yourself and your needs. Don't be a door-mat parent. Hold firm to limits that protect your rights and preserve your dignity. Children learn to value themselves when they live with parents who value themselves. Children develop a lack of courtesy and respect when they live with parents who cave in to their whims and wants.

> "I know you'd like half of my sandwich,
>   but I'm hungry and I intend to finish it.
>   You can make yourself one."
> "I'm enjoying the rocking chair right now,
>   you can have a turn when I am finished."
> "This program is important to me. It's over
>   at 5 o'clock."

OF POSITIVE PARENTING

In the following true story, a T.A.P.P. instructor safeguards her own needs but successfully keeps the interaction constructive by using the listening skills.

"After eight days of being kept inside with a sick child, I decided that my fever-free seven year old was well enough to accompany me to the rec center and sit by the pool for an hour while I swam and showered. I warned him that we would leave in about ten minutes and he might want to gather some books to take. This is a verbatim account of our conversation.

"Thanks to the listening skills, what might have turned into a power struggle became a constructive interaction."

Mother:
I'll help you get your shoes on so we can leave.
Tom:
I don't want to go.
Mother:
You still don't feel good.
Tom:
I feel all right but I'm not going.
Mother:
You really don't want to go.
Tom:
I want to watch T.V.
Mother:
You'd rather stay here.
Tom:
I want to stay home.
Mother:
Home is sometimes the best place to be.
Tom:
It sure is! (Finishes putting on shoes and heads for the car.)
Tom:
It was okay to come because you didn't make me come!"

The logic of Tom's final statement shows that he was allowed the space to retain his self-respect and that he felt as though he had participated in the decision. He did not feel forced. Whether or not they were going was never a question in the dialogue. The key to Tom's cooperation was hearing and reflecting his feelings. Thanks to the listening skills, what might have turned into a power struggle became a constructive interaction that set the stage for some quality time. (Courtesy Jo Ling and Tom.)

Good listening skills and quality time let children participate in discussions without interruption. In adult-child conversations, children are frustrated by parents who answer for them. When anyone asks your child a question **let him answer the question without interruption from you.** This shows respect. Whereas "take over" parents are saying. "You're incapable of telling this story as well as I can tell it." Instead, listen and respect your child's contributions, even when they are not what you would have liked them to be. This will enhance your relationship and contribute to the quality of the time you are spending together.

Children want to be thought of as capable and independent. Indeed, the child's need for independence is as strong as the child's need for love. It surfaces before the age of three. If unsatisfied, it propels the parent and child into a power struggle relationship. Parents can help satisfy this need by recognizing the contributions children make both to family discussions and to the work of the family. The work of the family is a built in opportunity for providing quality time. The work must be necessary work but need not be difficult. Participation in family work and in family discussions helps children feel responsible and worthwhile. It provides opportunities for quality interactions. Participation is vital if we are to move toward rather than away from our goals. Recognize the small but valuable actions that all children perform from time to time. Acknowledge the effort as well as the completed task. Let go of perfection -- don't add on warnings, lectures or criticism. Be specific.

"You picked up all the dirty clothes and separated the dark colors from the light. Your help made the washing job seem easy today!"

"You stayed right with the baby in his car seat while I carried the groceries in. You laughed and played with him and kept him happy. It was a big help to me."

Remember, the tasks should be necessary work, the comments specific, and the lessons on "how to" offered at another time.

In summary, constructive interactions that provide quality time depend on not using roadblocks and learning the listening skills. Listen to feelings and let your child know they have been heard. Deal constructively with accidental mishaps, look for opportunities for children to contribute to family discussions and to the

Recognize the small, but valuable actions that all children perform from time to time. "You stayed right with the baby in his car seat. It was a big help to me."

work of the family, respect and value your rights and dignity, don't interrupt your child's contributions and learn to be specific when commenting on their participation in family concerns.

Think of a time when you were a child that you feel really, really good about. You felt happy, proud, pretty, able, important. Remember exactly where you were, who you were with, and why you felt so special. This obviously involved a constructive interaction. This obviously was a quality time for you.

How can we help our children develop these kinds of good feelings about themselves? Write down at least five specific things you could practice to help your child feel special and to help you provide interactions that consist of quality time for you and your child.

LISTENING AND QUALITY TIME

Use the following situations for applying a listening response that will contribute to a constructive interaction.

Mother has denied fifteen year old Ann's request for money to purchase a new pair of jeans. Ann goes into a fit of rage. "You're awful, you never let me do anything. I hate you!"

Your response:

Kayla is three years old. After playing hard all day she is ready to settle down and watch her favorite show, Sesame Street to begin. Soon after Sesame Street begins, she falls asleep. When she wakes up, she discovers that

Sesame Street is over and she is very disappointed. She cries, screams, and demands that Mother put Sesame Street back on the T.V.

Your response:

_____

_____

_____

_____

_____

_____

Barbara is six years old. She has a brand new pair of party shoes. Barbara wants to wear them outside to show her friends how wonderful they are. It has been raining for days. It is not raining now but the yard is muddy and wet. The other kids are playing in the yard. She says, "They're my shoes and I want to wear them. Please Mom please, please, please!"

Your response:

_____

_____

_____

_____

_____

_____

Listening to feelings can open avenues of communication that would never have been reached. Dr. Thomas Gordon in *Parent Effectiveness Training* describes the experience of a skeptical father who had just learned the listening skills in one of his classes.

"I want to report to the class an amazing experience I had this week. My daughter Jean (15 yrs.) and I haven't said a civil word to each other for about two years, except maybe, 'Pass the bread,' or 'Can I have the salt and pepper?' The other night she and her boy friend were sitting at the table in the kitchen when I came home. I overheard my daughter telling her boy friend how much she hated school and how she was disgusted with most of her girl friends. I decided right then and there I would sit down and do nothing but listen, even if it killed me. Now, I'm not going to say I did a perfect job, but I surprised myself. I wasn't too bad. Well, will you believe it, they both started talking to me and never stopped for two hours. I learned more about my daughter and what she is like in those two hours than I had in the past five years. On top of that, the rest of the week she was downright friendly to me. What a change!"

"Through listening, I learned more about my daughter and what she is like in those two hours than I had in the past five years."

Listening does not always result in a final resolution or decision. **You can consider listening to be effective if you succeed in keeping communication open and if you succeed in resisting the roadblocks.** Sometimes the parent needs to set a limit because of time constraints or simply a need to guard her time alone. The following true story, from a former T.A.P.P. Instructor, is a good example of both the unresolved issue and setting an appropriate limit on listening while still maintaining an interaction that is constructive.

Katherine came in from school upset by a lunch room problem. Everyday another very popular girl in her class would "ditch" a place in the lunch line for herself and a small group of friends from Katherine.

Katherine:
I hate Mary Jane - she thinks she's such a big deal!
Mother:
Problems?
Katherine:
She always cheats on me in the lunch line and the other kids in back of me get mad at me.
Mother:
She "cheats" on you?
Katherine:
Yeah - she ditches in front of me and she usually brings Sue and Barbara too!
Mother:
And it gets you in trouble.
Katherine
Yeah - the kids in back of me get really mad.
Mother:
They get mad at you!
Katherine:
They sure do - and then Mary Jane never talks to me either - and she doesn't sit with me.
Mother:
And you feel pretty left out....
Katherine:
Well I don't have anybody to sit with.
Mother:
It's no fun sitting alone!
Katherine:
It sure isn't -- I hate that Mary Jane.
Mother:
[Pause....]..Hmm...well, what are you going to do about it? Do you have a plan?
Katherine:
No.

Mother did not give Katherine any advice nor did she continue the listening. The next day before school Katherine said - "Mom - I have a plan." Mother said - "Good", and had sense enough not to question Katherine about her plan but rather to let her accept responsibility for her own problem. (Courtesy Florence Mahoney & Katherine)

THE SELF-FULFILLING PROPHECY

Adele Faber and Elaine Mazlish in *How to Talk So Kids Will Listen And Listen So Kids Will Talk* discuss the self-fulfilling prophecy.

"Never underestimate the power of your words on a young person's life. Parents need to be warned of the dangers of labeling.

> 'My oldest is a problem child, the youngest is
>   a pleasure.'
> 'Bobby is a born bully.'
> 'Billy is a pushover, anyone can take advantage
>   of him.'
> 'I don't know what to feed Julie anymore.
>   She's such a picky eater.'
> 'It's a waste of money to buy anything new
>   for Rickie - He's so destructive. He'll just
>   tear it up.'

Children will walk in the footsteps we lay down for them. The child who has been given the name begins to play the game. The way a parent thinks about a child is the way that child will think about himself - and the way a child thinks about himself will affect his feelings and behavior. To free children from playing out an undesirable role, parents need to look for opportunities that will show the child a new picture of himself.

Be a storehouse for your child's special moments. Model the behavior you'd like to encourage and follow through with interactions that provide quality time for you and your child. Never underestimate the power of your words on a young person's life! " *

* *How to Talk So Kids Will Listen,* by Adele Faber and Elaine Mazlish.

PRACTICE MAKES PROGRESS

We now know that relationships between parents and children are strengthened or weakened through language. The words we use can make children feel worthless or feel worthwhile. Again, our first positive parenting skill is to unlearn a lifetime of damaging talk and replace it with responses that build self-esteem.

Instead of saying:

> "Big boys don't cry!"
> "Why don't you study more?"
> "You always forget your lunch!"
> "Did you ask them nicely?"

Try listening to feelings either (in your head) or "out loud":

> (He's afraid of the dog.)
> (She's worried about school.)
> "It's no fun to go without lunch!"
> "You'd really like to play with somebody."

Listening to feelings is a skill that can be learned. It strengthens relationships, builds self-esteem, helps children solve their own problems and contributes to the parent's sense of well being.

"You don't like your teacher!"
"You had a bad game!"
"It's no fun to sit alone."
"She's too young to jump rope."

Damaging talk (a roadblock) not only makes children feel worthless, it leads to criticism and negative prophecy.

"You're stupid."
"You dummy!"
"You never clean your room."
"You always forget your lunch!"

Blame and shame are useless! As Haim Ginott said, "When the milk spills - hand 'em a sponge!"

Before we move on to the third communication skill, let's explore more about the effect of parental attitude and language. I think all of us agree that children see themselves as we see them. This can work toward or against the child. Remember, a parent who says to himself "This child never sits still - the teachers will lose their minds!" - is likely to see that negative prophecy fulfilled.

On the other hand, if we can learn to treat the child as if he already is, what we would like him to become, he will experience positive prophecy and begin to build self esteem.

A child's concept of himself is not inborn... it is a result of how other persons have regarded him. Many of us have lived most of our lives surrounded by people who were critical of us; we learned to be critical of ourselves and have had a hard time building self esteem.

T
H
E

A
R
T

OF POSITIVE PARENTING

Dorothy Briggs in *Your Child's Self-Esteem - The Key to His Life* divides all of us into three categories: high self-esteem, the winners; mid self-esteem, the doubters; and low self-esteem, the losers. She points out that most of us, including the all "A" student, fall into the doubtful category.

Most often, according to Briggs, the parent's view of a child is the child's view of himself. Your critical attitude toward your child builds low self esteem. An accepting attitude builds high self esteem.

Stanley Coopersmith in a study called *The Antecedents of Self-Esteem*, agrees. His conclusions show that children build self-esteem when they feel total or near total acceptance by their parents. We are the most important factor in our children's lives. Both the words we use and the attitudes we develop are critical in building self-esteem.

To develop a nurturing attitude, try to understand the difference between what children need and what they want. After food, rest and shelter, children have important needs that can and should be met. Their wants are a bottomless pit. They want, for example, to have things done for them; they need to do for themselves. They want every toy advertised on television; they need friends to play with. The important needs are:

1. *To feel significant - to feel worthwhile.* **This is a need to contribute rather than receive - a need to give, not get - a need to participate, to make choices and to make decisions.**
2. *To belong - to feel secure.* In the early years, security comes from belonging to a family. As children grow, security also comes from making friends and finding a place in a community.
3. *To feel loved ---to be loved completely for*

46

themselves. To be loved no matter what they do or say or look like. It is a love that criticizes behavior not people. It is called unconditional love.

When these needs are not met, children feel worthless, left out and discouraged. When these needs are met, children thrive, feel worthwhile, make friends and learn to take care of themselves.

Haim Ginott in *Liberated Parents, Liberated Children* by Adele Faber and Elaine Mazlish takes us a step further in helping re-direct unacceptable behavior by building feelings of worth and acceptance: "The question now", Dr. Ginott said, "is how can we help a child change from undependable to dependable, from a mediocre student to a capable student, from someone who won't amount to very much to someone who will count for something. The answer is both simple and complicated: **We treat a child as if he already is what we would like him to become."**

Think a child a loser and he will lose for sure. Think a child a winner and he has a chance!

Children are typecast into many different roles. They see themselves through their parents' eyes. Winning roles need to be affirmed and reinforced. Losing roles are best ignored, and, if possible, forgotten. This is a challenging job! Learn to project your children into their best roles. Think of them as winners. **Instead of telling them what's wrong, catch them doing something right.**

In the following dialogue, the mother's listening responses turn a difficult situation into a constructive interaction that catches her child doing something right.

Molly came to her Mother and said, "Jenny said I wasn't her best friend anymore. She said that Barbara was her best friend and Susie White was her next best friend and that I wasn't even her third best friend....and that I'm not invited to her party either."

Nothing is more frustrating for a parent than a child without friends. Kids need friends and parents can help in three specific ways:

First and most important, recognize her feelings both "out loud" and (in your head).

> "It hurts to be left out. It makes you sad and
> mad at the same time - and disappointed
> about the party. Sounds like you're having a
> very tough day!" (She's feeling lost, alone,
> embarrassed, guilty and very angry.)

Second, resist solving the problem for your child.

> Don't reassure - "We'll have our own party."
> Don't suggest - "Why don't you call Mary?"
> Don't interfere - (I'll call her Mother.)
> Don't downgrade - "I never liked Jenny
>   anyway!" and above all
> Don't blame - "What did you do to Jenny?"

Third, at a different time, encourage your child's "making friends" behaviors by noticing the things that she is doing right.

> "I really liked the way you shared your bike
>   last week when your cousins were here."
> "It was very nice to see you introduce our
>   new neighbor to the other kids. I bet it
>   made him feel like he belongs."

As you can see, the words we use with children are an important factor in building self-esteem. Instead of using the familiar roadblocking responses, we can learn to listen with full attention, pause before we respond, repeat back or re-state what the other person has said, give the feeling a name, respond with one word, "Hmmm", use a "you really wish" response, write a note or, instead of telling them what they're doing wrong, catch them doing something right. **Whether the problem is solved or not, the listening skills are successful when the lines of communication remain open and the interaction feels constructive.**

In the next story, a positive parent again turns a difficult situation into a constructive interaction. Tommy had a habit of telling his parents things that weren't true. He was trying to avoid the consequences of parental anger. Sometimes children simply believe that the truth is too unpleasant for parents to hear!

(I hate my baby brother, but I better not say so!)

Sometimes they simply believe in their own wishful thinking.

"The teacher said I was the best reader in the group!"

And sometimes they are responding to questions that trap them into telling lies.

"My new sweater is at school."

Tommy's Mother, when faced with a lie, is factual and direct without down-grading her child.

"New babies are sure hard to be around all the time!"

OF POSITIVE PARENTING

She is not afraid to allow in fantasy what doesn't exist in reality.

"You wish you were the best reader in the group!"

And when she already knows the answer, she doesn't ask the question! Such as: "Did you lose your new sweater?"

Sometimes, we trap children into telling lies: "Tommy just loves his baby brother!"

*Children develop courtesy and respect
when they live with parents who value themselves.*

*Children develop a lack of courtesy and respect
when they live with parents who
cave in to their whims and wants.*

When The Parent Owns The Problem

THE LANGUAGE OF DESCRIPTION

In Chapter One and Chapter Two, we've talked about several ways to help children who are feeling bad or discouraged or angry or disappointed. These skills help build self esteem and mutual respect. They also help make each parent-child interaction a constructive one. This section is designed to help parents share their own bad feelings and begin to redirect the child's unacceptable behavior when the problem belongs to the parent.

Language has two parts: listening and expressing. We've talked about listening to other people's feelings - now we are ready to introduce the language of description. Describe...what you see and how you feel.

Use words that describe instead of words that evaluate: "I see a purple house..."

Haim Ginott said - "I'm trying to teach parents a new language to use with children. I'm trying to teach them to use words that describe instead of words that evaluate. Words that evaluate hinder a child - words that describe set him free. Descriptive words also invite a child to work out his own solutions. Recently a little girl in my play room brought me a painting and said "Is it good?" I looked at it and answered, "I see a purple house, a red sun, a striped sky and lots of flowers. It makes me feel like I am in the country." She smiled and said, "I'm going to make another!"

I can guarantee you if Dr. Ginott had said "It's beautiful!" --the little girl would have said "Are you sure?" - Words that evaluate hinder a child -- words that describe set him free. Children need a clear and positive picture of themselves. Global praise like "good" - "wonderful" - "perfect" - "fantastic" raises doubt and creates anxiety. Global words cloud a child's image and interrupt his progress. Instead, observe carefully your child's competencies and contributions - then praise the action rather than the child.

For example, when a toddler manages to open or close a door, to feed himself with a spoon or to put on a shoe, our "good girl" "big boy" is a judgment response. It evaluates the worth of the person rather than the competency of the behavior. How much better to say "Well done!"

"Well done" speaks to the behavior, to the deed, to the action. It gives the child a feeling of accomplishment. It helps the child feel capable and worthwhile about what he has achieved. It sets the child free to try new things and to learn new skills without being judged as "good" or "bad". "Well done" uses Dr. Ginott's language of description.

Some additional examples:

"You've worked all weekend on finishing
    that book and writing the report. I'm
    impressed with your discipline!"
The child thinks: "I like to finish my school
    work on time."

"Your hands and face are clean and your hair
    is brushed. You look ready for company!"
The child thinks: "I take care of myself!"

Describe what you see....describe how you feel.

LISTEN TO FEELINGS - YOURS AND YOUR CHILD'S

Both love and anger are successfully expressed through the language of description. When the parent has a problem, he/she (you) needs to sort out true feelings and examine them. Suppose a child is eating a popsicle and starts to sit on your newly slipcovered chair; or a child is opening a package that you just wrapped for mailing; or a child is interrupting your telephone conversation with the baby's doctor. These situations will feel differently to each of us. Some of us will be able to change the way we feel about the problem, that is say to ourselves, "She's only four years old and loves to open packages." Some of us will be able to change the environment to suit the child, that is, telephone the doctor after you have found an activity for your child to explore. But some of us will need to respect the feelings we have about the problem and learn to share them in the language of description.

In Chapter IX of *Liberated Parents* the authors have twice repeated Dr. Ginott's statements regarding parent's feelings. "A parent should respect his own limits." .... "It is important to accept the reality of our feelings of the moment.".... "It's best to be authentic with our children."

The difficulty for parents is... we don't always know what we feel. And there is usually a discrepancy between what we really feel and what we have been told we should feel. For example:

"My children wanted to go to a movie. They were too young to go alone. My husband said 'No - I'm watching the ball game.' The kids came to me. They pleaded and begged. I was planning to sew all afternoon but gave in to their pleas. I was disappointed in losing my free time and resented the effort I was making. I was cross with them and critical of everything that happened. We all had a miserable time. It would have been much better for all of us if I could have been authentic about my feelings too."

In another household, the mother might have been able to alter the environment by renting a movie for the kids, or change the way she feels about the problem and enjoying the movie with the kids. **There is no right or wrong way.** The important thing to remember is don't judge yourself harshly if your feelings are authentic.

To be successful, the language of description needs your real feeling.

Getting in touch with your *real* feeling instead of paying attention to your "should" feeling is the much healthier and constructive reaction.... and your children will learn that your needs and wants are to be respected....and that it's O.K. to respect yourself. The hard part is they won't learn this overnight but rather over time. One of the most important *Tips from T.A.P.P.* says, "Don't be a 'peace at any price' parent. Hold firm to limits that protect your rights and preserve your dignity. Children develop courtesy and respect when they live with parents who value themselves. Children develop a lack of courtesy and respect when they live with parents who cave in to their whims and wants."

The skill we are introducing in this section is to learn to sort out our true feelings and express them in a language of description. Accept the fact that in the natural course of family life, our children will make us feel uncomfortable, annoyed, irritated, angry and furious. Recognize that you are entitled to these feelings without guilt, regret or shame.

Learn to express angry feelings without attacking personality or character. Describe clearly what you see, how you feel and how you are affected.

This is a delicate process. It does not necessarily

change behavior and it may cause conflict. It can, however, be a step toward solving family problems. The third skill is:

> **Describe what you see.**
> **Describe how you feel.**

Do not attack the other person and be ready to listen to their side of the story with a listening response. When you give your child a descriptive message about unacceptable behavior, be ready to make a quick shift to a listening, understanding response. This says, "I expect you to care about my feelings and my point of view because I care about yours." Thomas Gordon in *Parent Effectiveness Training.* calls it "Shifting Gears".

Dad:
"I'm worried about the water on the bathroom floor - I'm afraid someone will get hurt!"
Bobby:
"Every time I wash my hair, the shower curtain blows open and the water sprays all over - It isn't heavy enough!"
Dad:
"You think the shower curtain doesn't do a good job."
Bobby:
"It should be heavier - it won't stay down - but I'll dry the water with a towel when I'm finished."
Dad:
"Thanks - I'd appreciate it - and I'll see if I can weight the shower curtain with some of my fishing sinkers."

Children will respond to your message with less resistance if their feelings are heard with respect. Shifting from a descriptive message to a listening response demonstrates respect.

Sometimes it helps to describe how to take care of the problem.

> "When I see clothes and books all over this
> room, I feel angry, frustrated and disappointed!
> The rule is, personal belongings belong in
> your bedroom."
>
> "When there's water all over the bathroom
> floor, I'm afraid someone will fall and it
> might be me! Dry it with a towel -- put
> the towel in the wash!"

Sometimes, you can change the environment.

Fix the shower curtain or install a shower door.

Sometimes, you can change the way you feel about the problem.

> Say to yourself, [A little water on the floor
> is not a big deal].

But sometimes, the feelings you have about the problem need to be expressed to your child.

Remember, concentrate on what you see and how you feel. Describe behavior -- not people! Haim Ginott tells us, "You can act a little bit nicer than you feel but not much!" He cautions parents to direct their anger toward the deed and not the doer....toward the misbehavior and not the child....and to use words that describe instead of words that evaluate. For example: "I'm worried about your library fine!" vs. "You are so careless about your library books. I'm ashamed of you!"

I once saw a mental health poster that would be a good motto for all parents. It said "Learn to show your anger at the time you are angry. Make it clear what you're angry about. It's O.K. to have angry feelings - it's O.K. to name angry feelings - it's O.K. to show angry feelings, as long as no one gets hurt." Learning to express angry feelings appropriately is worth working on. None of us are adept at this. Ginott says "It is the work of a lifetime!"

So - when faced with unacceptable behavior, examine the alternatives. Change the environment, change the way you feel about the problem or use a message of description. Criticize behavior, not people! And if talking will get you in trouble, write a note. This gives you time to pause and listen to your own bad feelings before you deliver the message.

Sometimes, parents are caught with unexpected feelings that cause an instant angry reaction. The first feeling is often fear or worry, the second feeling is anger. Whether twelve or twenty, the child needs to hear a parent message that conveys the first feeling rather than the anger. Sharing your first feeling causes remorse. "I am angry" causes resentment. For example, when children come home later than they are expected. "I was worried to death about you. I didn't know where you were or how to reach you!" is a healthier reaction than blame or scolding. Blame and scolding reflect the anger rather than your primary feelings of fear and worry.

Make it clear what you're angry about. "Snakes make me feel sick and worried and scared to death!"

After all when faced with unacceptable behavior parents want to instill remorse not revenge. The road-blocks, especially the obvious ones, instill revenge. Children take on additional bad feelings. They plot to get even and harbor feelings that hurt your relationship and hurt self-esteem.

WHOSE PROBLEM IS IT?

Parents need to recognize problem ownership before they know which skill, the Listening or the Language of Description, to use.

Sometimes problems belong to the child, sometimes to the parent and sometimes to both parent and child.

When the problem belongs to the child, that is, it does not interfere with the parent's rights or dignity or with health and safety, use the listening skill and trust that your child can find his own solutions, solve his own problems and learn from his own mistakes.

When the problem belongs to the parent, that is, **you feel strongly** that it does interfere with your rights or dignity or with health and safety use the language of description. Describe what you see, describe how you feel and how to take care of the problem.

Chapter Four introduces some skills that will help resolve problems that belong to both parent and child.

In the following exercise, if it's the child's problem, use listening. If it's the parent's problem, use a language of description. If it's a problem for both, we'll talk about some additional skills in Chapter Four.

Search out your true, basic feeling...then write an acceptable, positive response to your child using the skills you have learned so far.

To prepare for the following exercise, remember both the listening skill and the language of description.

For listening:--Sometimes it's easy to figure out what a child is feeling but sometimes it isn't - people, especially children, speak in codes.

"I hate you!" -- probably means you have just told him he couldn't do something he wanted to do.

"I'm going to drop History" --may mean he's worried about History, and it may mean he hates the teacher.

The child falls, her knee is bloody, she is crying and says "Look at all that blood!" She may be hurt, scared of blood or embarrassed that she fell in front of the other kids. Don't be afraid to guess at the feeling because the child will straighten you out if you're wrong!

When the Child Owns the Problem:

Ask yourself, does this action interfere with my rights or dignity or with health or safety? If the answer is "no", let go. The problem belongs to the child!
Listen to Feelings...then frame a positive response.

10 yrs.

1. When my child forgets his lunch money,
   I feel...
   My response to my child..
   ....

8 yrs.

2. When my child doesn't get a part in the
   school play,
   I feel...
   My response to my child..
   ....

15 yrs.

3. When my child is left out of the game,
   I feel...
   My response to my child..
   ....

8 yrs..

4. When my child fights with his best friend,
   I feel...

My response to my child...

....

16 yrs.

5. When my child doesn't have a date for the school prom,
   I feel...
   My response to my child...

   ....

13 yrs.

6. When my child doesn't make the team,
   I feel...
   My response to my child...

   ....

9 yrs.

7. When my child's team loses a game,
   I feel...
   My response to my child...

   ....

11 yrs.

8. When my child gets yelled at in school,
   I feel...
   My response to my child...

   ....

7 yrs.

9. When my child's best friend moves away,
   I feel...
   My response to my child...

   ....

14 yrs.

10. When my child hates his haircut,
    I feel...
    My response to my child...

    ....

When the Parent Owns the Problem:

Ask yourself, does this action interfere with my rights or dignity or with health or safety? If the answer is "yes" then describe! Be authentic! The problem belongs to you!

Describe what you see, describe how you feel. Then give a positive response.

6 yrs.

1. When my child crayons all over my wallpaper,

    I feel...

    My response to my child...

    ....

11 yrs.

2. When my child uses tough language,

    I feel...

    My response to my child...

    ....

8 yrs.

3. When my child doesn't come home on time,

    I feel...

    My response to my child...

    ....

15 yrs.

4. When my child borrows my sweater and ruins it,

    I feel...

    My response to my child...

    ....

17 yrs.

5. When my child loses my car keys,

    I feel...

    My response to my child...

    ....

7 yrs.

6. When my child whines and complains all the time
   I feel...
   My response to my child...

   ....

10 yrs.

7. When my child forgets to empty the trash,
   I feel...
   My response to my child...

   ....

4 yrs..

8. When my child loses one new shoe,
   I feel...
   My response to my child...

   ....

3 yrs.

9. When my child won't go to bed at night,
   I feel...
   My response to my child...

   ....

18 yrs..

10. When my child brings a pet snake home from school,
    I feel..
    My response to my child..

    ....

Review your responses to be sure you have not used a roadblock. Be especially careful of the roadblocks that are not obvious. Usually, the shorter the response, the better. Whenever possible, replace a paragraph with a sentence and a sentence with a word.

Ask:

How would my child feel about my response?
Would my response lead to further argument?

Would my response stop communication
altogether?
Has this interaction been as constructive
as possible?

If your responses are not working in real life, **part
of the problem may be in what has happened to you
before the interaction begins.**

How are you feeling?
What are your needs?
Is there too much to do and too little time?
Are you showing respect for his feelings?
Are you using roadblocks to communicate
with your child?
Is there something about your behavior that
contributes to your child's unacceptable
behavior?

Recently, a father in one of our T.A.P.P.
classes reported the following story about parent behavior contributing to the problem:
"Matt, my six-year old became very
upset when he couldn't find the soccer jersey
which he had placed on his dresser the previous
night. He came to me and said, 'I really need
that jersey.' Trying to apply what I had learned
in this class, I responded, 'Sounds like you're
worried that you won't be able to play in your
game if you don't have a jersey on Saturday.' At
that point, he seemed to calm down a little and
there was a moment of silence. In retrospect, I probably
should have kept my mouth shut, but because of the
silence and my uncontrollable need to offer solutions, I
committed an error that immediately escalated a situation

*How easy it is to
take a situation and
escalate it into some-
thing much worse.*

which was under control. When I posed the question 'What do you think happened to your jersey,' he immediately responded that his four year old brother, John, had probably taken it. I challenged this assertion and told him that he always blames his brother when he can't find something. In a matter of seconds, the search for a soccer jersey had turned into a full-blown argument over his relationship with his brother. In trying to find out what went wrong, I realized how easy it is to take a situation and escalate it into something much worse. It is a lesson that has made me much more conscious of my tendency to contribute to the mayhem around our house!"

And part of the problem may be a conflict of values. The parent, for example, wants some semblance of cleanliness, order and quiet -- things that most children don't care about. Children often prefer noise and confusion. Parents who are too rigid about their values, may want to try to show respect for the child's values The more rigid the parent remains, the more actively the child will resist. The parent becomes the enemy -- always making the child do what he doesn't want to do. The child's attitude becomes "I'll do what I want." The parent's attitude becomes "You'll do as I say." And the battle begins.

Instead, when faced with your child's unacceptable behavior, be brief, offer choices, separate the deed from the doer, match the language of anger to the mood of the moment....that is....be authentic and don't be afraid to show respect for your child's values. Remember, values are handed down most effectively through modeling, not lecturing, criticizing or arguing. (More about this in Chapter Six.)

Hints that might help one of the most often reported parent owned problems are offered in the following *Tip from T.A.P.P.*

Bedtime: The All-night Affair

Small children need a routine and a schedule at bed-time, but are often skilled at prolonging the day, engaging the parent and making bedtime an all-night affair.

Hints that might help:

- Talk about your feelings and needs not about your child's unacceptable behavior. "I'm tired and I need time for myself now!" "I'm frustrated! I have work to do and I need to be alone!"
- Establish a familiar bedtime routine that is geared toward winding down: a warm bath, a back rub, a story, a glass of water and into bed with the door closed.
- Pick a reasonable bedtime hour and stick with it, but be flexible about what happens in the room if your child is unable to sleep. For example, he can talk to the animals, look at a book, listen to music -- quiet things that can be done in bed.
- Expect that he can go to sleep by himself and tell him about it. "I'm so happy you know how to go to sleep by yourself." Acknowledge it when he does.
- Satisfy his need for your time and attention at other times of the day: play games, tell stories, take walks, interact together instead of side by side.
- Make sure his need for independence is fulfilled. Everyday, ask yourself, "What am I doing for my child that he could be doing for himself?" Offer choices, and let him make decisions that truly affect his life.
- And most important, during the daytime

hours, give encouragement. Instead of telling him what's wrong, catch him doing something right.

Another problem that parents often ask about in the T.A.P.P. classes concerns cooperation on household

The father and often the mother worked with them side by side.

chores. Cooperation can be successful when families work together and when children are involved in decision making. I am reminded of a family that lived across the street for most of the time they were raising three boys. The boys cut the grass and cleaned the yard every Friday afternoon in the summer. In the fall, they raked leaves and cleaned gutters and in the spring, they helped plant flowers and again cut the grass and cleaned the sidewalks and driveway. During snowy winters, they not only cleaned the snow from their own driveway and walks but also cleaned the walks for the next door neighbor, a widow who lived alone. I never heard the parents raise their voices or plead or beg or chastise for a job poorly done. I also never saw the boys working alone. The father and often the mother worked with them side by side. The family seemed to accept their chores as a necessary part of family living. Cooperation can be successful when parents and children work together, and when children are involved in decision making and problem solving.

ENCOURAGEMENT

Children who misbehave need encouragement more than they need correction.

Children misbehave for a reason. They misbehave because they have a need that is not being met. The real needs are food, rest, shelter, to feel worthwhile, secure, loved and accepted. When real needs are not met, children misbehave to fill mistaken needs.

The mistaken needs are attention (to be noticed), power (to fight), revenge (to get even), and avoidance (to give up). * 1.

Children who misbehave to fill mistaken needs are more successfully redirected through encouragement than correction.

Some guidelines for encouragement are:

1. Catch your child doing something right.
2. Tell him about it.
3. Hug him when you tell him.
4. Tell him how good you feel about what he did.
5. Encourage your child to do the same for you. * 2.

* 1. Rudolf Dreikurs, M.D., *Children The Challenge*
* 2. Spencer Johnson, M.D., *The One-Minute Mother*

In this chapter, we have explored the importance of parental attitude and language. The words we use with children and how we feel about our children influence and impact their self-esteem. Children need to feel important, loved and accepted. Parents need to catch them doing something right. Parents also need to avoid global praise and to praise the deed, not the doer.

Recognize problem ownership. If it's the child's problem, use listening. If the problem belongs to the parent, you can sometimes change the environment or change the way you feel about the problem, but when you have strong feelings, be authentic and honor those feelings appropriately. Describe what you see and how you feel. Describe behavior not people, and try to determine and share your primary feelings. Be ready to shift gears and listen to your child's feelings when you deliver your message of description. Don't let your behavior escalate a budding situation. Bedtime problems need special efforts and chores need parent child cooperation and participation in decision making. Above all, stop using roadblocks. They increase rather than reduce the number of problems that belong to the parent. Finally, instead of telling children what they're doing wrong, catch them doing something right and tell them about it.

MORE PRACTICE...MORE PROGRESS

In Chapters One and Two, we have learned about the important connection between feelings and behavior. Good feelings thrive on listening and acceptance; bad feelings thrive on the traditional responses people use with people, the roadblocks.

They are:

Blaming
Shaming
Name Calling
Threatening
Commanding
Negative Prophecy
Suggesting solutions
Reassuring

Probing with questions

Global, non-specific praise.

Lecturing - that is teaching little moral lessons
by telling kids what's wrong and how to
correct it instead of listening to feelings.

Roadblocks stop communication and hurt self
esteem. Roadblocks are an attempt to control the child by
directing what he should or should not do. This is demon-
strated in the following dialogue:

Child:

My teacher really yelled at me in gym today.

Father:

Well what was that about? What did you do?

Child:

I didn't serve the ball right. I've never played vol-
ley ball before. It wasn't my fault!

Father:

You never learned to listen to your teachers. You
need to do what they say to do.

Child:

It wasn't my fault. She didn't teach us how to
serve. How was I supposed to know? And she
yelled in front of the whole class!

Father:

I think if you played outside more, you'd be a better vol-
ley ball player and better at other sports too.

*"Learn to listen with-
out approval or disap-
proval -- without praise
or criticism." -H. Ginott*

Re-write this dialogue with listening responses.
Keep your goals in mind. Don't let the conversation turn
into an argument. Let your child share her feelings about
the experience and begin to accept responsibility for her own
problems. Remember, when feelings are denied, parent and
child become increasingly hostile toward each other. Use the

listening responses through silence, naming the feeling, restating what the child has said, answering with a non judgmental word. "Oh?", "Wow", "Mmm" or using "You wish", such as,"You wish you were a better player!"

Child:
My teacher really yelled at me in gym today!

Father:

_____

_____

Child:

_____

_____

Father:

_____

_____

Child:

_____

_____

Real listening is hard work, it involves much more than waiting for a child to quit talking so you can say what you want to say. It involves resisting the urge to offer solutions and advice.

In this chapter, we have explored how to communicate our own bad feelings through using a language of description.

Describe what you see, describe how you feel. And when you blow it, don't be afraid to play *erase*, and start again. "I'm sorry I said that!. Let's *erase* and start again." Children are very forgiving. They will be happy to give you another chance. We can learn about forgiveness from them.

In Chapter Four, we will concentrate on behavior that is ultimately a problem for both parent and child. We will introduce skills for solving conflict and redirecting children's behavior. We will learn about the difference between discipline and punishment, a word about rules, and some effective tools parents can use to re-direct children's misbehavior.

First, more about children's needs. When real needs (food, rest, shelter, to feel worthwhile, secure, loved and accepted) are not met, children misbehave to fill mistaken needs. Each mistaken need is different and each needs a different specific action to successfully redirect the child's behavior.

If the child's mistaken need is attention - to be noticed - the recommended parent response is to ignore.

If the child's mistaken need is power - to fight - the recommended parent response is withdraw from the conflict, don't engage. For example, a child looking for a fight might say "You never give me any stars!, you always blame me!" - trying to engage the parent in a power struggle. Resist entering the battle!. Dis-engage from the conversation completely or use a listening response that concentrates on how the child feels rather than a defense or a rational explanation which will keep you engaged in the fight. For example: - "You're feeling cheated!"

If the child's need is revenge - to get even - avoid punishment! Punishment will increase the feelings of revenge and cause the child to "get even" in more creative ways.

OF POSITIVE PARENTING

If the child's need is avoidance - to give up - the parent must refrain from coaxing or from doing it for him. Instead, concentrate on what the child has accomplished. Catch him doing something right!

Remember, children move back and forth between these needs. And most children display more than one need at a time.

Four Reasons Children Misbehave

Child Wants	Child Behaves	Child's Real Need	Recommended Parent Response
Attention	Begs, whines, misbehaves. "Please Mom, Please, please	To feel important, accepted and loved. To belong and to contribute.	Listen. Share feelings. Set firm limits. Problem solve. Give responsibility.
Power	Bossy. Causes trouble. "Make me!" "I am the boss."	"	Don't fight. Problem solve. Share feelings. Stop using roadblocks Listen!
Revenge	Angry. Gets even. Feels blamed. Blames others.	"	Encourage. Problem solve. Share feelings. Listen.
Avoidance	Afraid of failure "I can't." "I don't know how!"	"	Train and encourage. Don't deny feelings Arrange small successes. Use communication skills. Give responsibility.

Children move back and forth between these mistaken needs. You may see your child in more than one category. The real needs, however, remain the same. To feel loved, accepted, important and have a sense of "belonging!"

Children need discipline...
and parents need methods of discipline that work.

Punishment is not one of them.

Peace At Last!

PROBLEM OWNERSHIP

Problem ownership is a complicated issue. Sometimes the problem belongs clearly to the parent or to the child, but sometimes the problem belongs first to the parent and then to both, or first to the child and then to both. For example, everyday when Mom comes home from work, the kitchen is a mess. The peanut butter jar is open and on the counter, the bread is half sliced and has not been put away, empty milk glasses are in the sink not rinsed, the milk carton is still open and not refrigerated and banana peels and apple cores are decaying rapidly instead of in the disposal. These conditions are not a problem for the child until Mom gives a strong message about what she sees and how she feels. Conversely, school problems belong exclusively to the child until the teacher asks the parent to intervene and supervise a solution, or until the report card full of failing grades is presented for inspection.

In this section, we will discuss problems such as these and the choices parents can effectively use to redirect children's behavior. Recognizing problem ownership will help pinpoint the preferred positive parenting skill. Recognizing the effects of punishment will be a motivation to try a positive parenting skill instead of punishment.

PUNISHMENT - DOES IT WORK?

The following exercise may help you remember that punishment is not an effective deterrent to misbehavior.

Exercise:

Remember a time when you were a child, when you were punished for something. How were you punished? For what? Did you change - did it work? How did the punishment make you feel? Share this experience with other family members or with a close, non-judgmental friend.

If you clear your mind completely, then say "discipline!", what is the first word association that comes to mind? Ready? "Discipline."

Don't be discouraged if your word association is "punishment!" I'm convinced there is a confusion in our society between the word "discipline" and the word "punishment." The synonym for discipline is teaching - not punishment. It comes from the Latin word disciple -- or teacher. The purpose of discipline is to help children become contributing members of society. The end goal of discipline is self- discipline --- self-regulation. Parents want to raise children who accept responsibility for themselves.

Children need discipline! Children need discipline in order to live smoothly in the social order of the family -- to help themselves become self-regulated -- and to meet their needs without running roughshod over the needs of others.

Parents need discipline for the same reasons.

Children can be disciplined through the use of power and punishment or through methods that foster mutual respect and high self-esteem.

Let's briefly explore the results of power and punishment. Power and punishment make children feel either dependent, fearful and worthless .....or full of revenge and rebellion. In a caring relationship, there is no room for punishment.

Punishment, when it works, works with those children who need it the least. In other words, the submissive, shy, "good" child is easily punished into behavior change. But, at what cost? As a result of being punished, this child will suffer from feelings of fear, dependency and worthlessness.

For most children, punishment does not encourage behavior change but rather generates feelings of revenge and rebellion. Usually, the child says to himself: "I'll get even!" -- And they do! Kids are very adept at revenge.

Punishment may help parents control their children, it does not help children control themselves.

So.... how can parents discipline successfully and effectively, that is, re-direct behavior and generate feelings of worth and self-esteem.

Children can be disciplined successfully by parents who treat them with respect. Dr. Hugh Missildine in his book *Your Inner Child of the Past* states,

"Set firm limits when your child's actions interfere with your rights or dignity or with health or safety. Otherwise, let him go about the things that are his. Give no anxious warnings, threats, lectures, criticisms or comparisons." (The Roadblocks.)

Following this good advice, when a child's actions interfere with health and safety or with the rights and dignity of the parent or the social order of the household, children can be disciplined successfully with the following skills or tools: Limit - Choice - Action, Natural Consequences, High Expectations, Problem Solving and surprisingly, Modeling.

But if the child's actions do not interfere, the skills we are about to learn will not be effective. The parent must learn to let go.....to treat the child as an equal person, deserving of respect. As Dr. Missildine recommends, **"Let him go about the things that are his".**

LIMIT-CHOICE-ACTION

When faced with children's misbehavior, parents need to ask themselves some hard questions:

1. What is happening with me?
2. What am I afraid of?
3. **Have I done something to encourage this behavior?**
4. Does this behavior interfere with my rights or my dignity?
5. Does this behavior interfere with health and safety?

If the answer to (3.) is "Yes", the parent, may need to examine his own fears....to listen to the child's feelings - without interruption.... and to let go!

If the answer to (4.) and (5.) is "Yes" the parent can successfully set limits, a method of discipline we are about to learn, **providing the parent has stopped using roadblocks and has learned to listen to feelings.**

To determine which skill is most effective for each circumstance, review problem ownership. As we now know, sometimes problems belong to the child, sometimes to the parent and sometimes to both parent and child.

When the problem belongs to the child, that is, it does *not* interfere with your rights or dignity or with health and safety, use listening.

When the problem *does* interfere with your rights with dignity or with health and safety, **set fair but firm** limits, give choices not threats, and do what you say you will do.

When the problem persists, it then belongs to both parent and child and needs problem solving, a skill described later in this chapter.

When the child's behavior interferes with rights, dignity or health and safety, children can be successfully disciplined by Limit-Choice-Action if the parent has developed respect for the child.

Respect depends on learning to listen to feelings and using words that describe instead of words that evaluate, the skills from Chapters One, Two and Three.

Without respect -- limits, rules and consequences turn into punishment -- and the problem solving formulas fall apart.

A word about rules: Montessori said "The fewer the better"-- and there is an argument for that. Too many rules in the family, turn the parent into a police officer. However, in successful family living, some reasonable rules are almost always necessary.

Reasonable rules are rules that safeguard :
1. the social order of the family,
2. the health and safety of a person, and
3. the laws of the land.

1. Actions that jeopardize the social order of the family result in reasonable rules -- and should be followed by adult and child alike.
    "Tools belong in the tool box."
    "Car keys get returned to their owner."
    "He who snacks, cleans up!"
    "Personal belongings belong in your bedroom."

2. Actions that jeopardize the health and safety
   of a person result in reasonable rules and can
   be applied developmentally.
   > At any age, "No running in the
   > supermarket."
   > At age 3 and 4 and perhaps 5, "No bike
   > riding in the street."
   > At age 9, "No bike riding on Main Street."

3. Actions that break the laws of the land result
   in reasonable rules, and should be observed
   by adult and child alike.
   > "Follow the driving speed limits."
   > "No drinking under age 18."
   > "No teenage parties without parents at
   > home."
   > "No littering on streets and highways."

Ask Yourself :

> What's best for this family?
> Is this rule necessary?
> Does it cause more hassle than it's worth?
> Could it be designed in a democratic fashion,
> that is, giving the child equal voice in
> making the rule?
> Can the rule be eliminated all together?

Make a list of the rules in your house. Review your
list carefully. Put a + sign next to those rules that work
without conflict. Put a – sign next to the rules that cause
conflict. Examine the – rules carefully. Eliminate them if
you can. Save the rest for problem solving, a skill
described later in this section.

Rules:

_____

_____

_____

_____

_____

_____

_____

_____

_____

_____

When the problem interferes with the rights or dignity of the parent or with health and safety, we can successfully set limits that safeguard our rules. Make sure your rules are reasonable. State your rules early and often. Be brief, fair, firm and friendly.

Then:

Set a limit, offer a choice (one or several acceptable choices and one related to the limit), then take action - that is, **do what you say you will do**!

Here's how it works:

The Limit
"Tools must be returned and put away."

The Choice
"You can borrow my tools and return them or give up the privilege of using them. You decide."

The Action
"The tools are locked up this week. We'll try again next week."

Another example:

The Limit
"No bike riding in the street."

The Choice
"You can ride your bike on the sidewalk or in the yard but not in the street.

The Action
"The bike gets put away today, we'll try again tomorrow."

Keep the time related to the age of the child, (for a three year old you might say "we'll try again after lunch!") ...and the action related to the limit .

The success of this process depends on the action. Setting a limit and offering a choice without taking action will be regarded as a threat.

Above all - avoid using roadblocks - they undermine respect.

Limit-Choice-Action is a skill that has possibilities and problems. Before we introduce additional methods of discipline that work, we need to understand when Limit-Choice-Action is effective and when it causes negative consequences by leading into a power struggle.

Limit-Choice-Action is most effective when the conflict is a health and safety issue, or when the problem is a social order problem that *truly* belongs to the parent....by interfering with the parent's rights or dignity.

Social order problems that belong to both parent and child are resolved successfully only when the child agrees or buys into the solution or limit through problem solving, or, if the child experiences and doesn't like the natural consequences of his behavior.

Because Limit-Choice-Action is a skill that relies on the parent imposing a limit that the child may or may not accept, using this skill inappropriately leads to a power struggle, and power struggles create rather than solve family problems.

When the problem belongs primarily to the child but affects the life of the parent, Limit-Choice-Action is not an effective method of discipline. Learn to use problem solving instead.

The following examples demonstrate a Limit-Choice-Action that will predictably work and one that will probably lead to a power struggle. One of the following situations needs problem solving, a skill described later in this chapter.

Why does Limit-Choice-Action work in one example but not in the other?

1st. Example:
For the fourth time in a month, the parent cannot find his long nose pliers. He finally locates the pliers, uses them and locks the tool box. The parent then sets.....

The Limit
Tools must be returned and put away!

The Choice
You can borrow my tools and return them or give up the privilege of using them. You decide.

The Action
The tools are locked up today. We'll try again next weekend.

Second Example:
The child's teacher has complained the he never turns in completed homework. The parent sets:

The Limit
Homework gets finished and turned in every day.

The Choice
"You can do your homework right after school or after dinner during your television time, you decide."

The Action
"No television tonight. It's time for homework, you can choose again tomorrow."

Can you feel the difference in these two situations?

_____

Which situation needs problem solving?

_____

 Why?

_____
_____
_____
_____
_____

   The following work sheet will give you some practice in setting appropriate limits. Use behaviors that truly interfere with your rights, your dignity, or with health and safety.

The Action

The Choice

The Limit

The Behavior

High Expectations -
Expect That They Can...
Expect That They Will

The way a parent thinks about a child affects the way a child thinks about himself. A parent can shape a child's self image for better or worse through how he views and treats his child. A child will see himself as independent and capable when his parents see him and treat him as independent and capable. Conversely, labels that insult, criticize and blame can be devastating. Parents need to be warned of the dangers of the self-fulfilling prophecy. When the milk spills, or the lamp breaks, or the lunch is forgotten, the child who is called clumsy, stupid or forgetful will think of himself as clumsy, stupid or forgetful. And the behavior we are trying to change is reinforced instead. When the milk spills, a positive parent hands the child a sponge. This action says, "I see you as a person who is capable of helping himself." This action says "In time of trouble, we don't blame, we focus on solutions."

Children need to feel their own strength, to solve their own problems, to see themselves as independent and capable. **Parents can help by having high expectations that their children are responsible, independent and capable human beings.**

A child can rarely disagree with his parent's expectations. If you think a child a loser, he will lose for sure, and feel bad about himself. If you think a child a winner, he stands a chance.

As we learned in Chapter Two, this alternative for changing the overall behavior of a child is outlined very effectively in *Liberated Parents Liberated Children.*

"The question now is, how can we help a child change from undependable to dependable, from mediocre to capable, from someone who won't amount to very much to someone who will count for something. The answer is both simple and complicated. We treat him as if he already is what we would like him to become."

A parent from one of our classes reports:

"My child forgets everything. She leaves things at home that belong at school and leaves things at school that belong at home. Last week, she lost a new sweater, forgot to take her gym shoes to school on gym day, and she always forgets her lunch money. I was at my wits end! After our third T.A.P.P. class, I really tried to start treating her as if she were always responsible. We had no overnight miracles, but last week she ran back from the corner, grabbed her gym shoes, said 'I forgot again', and hurried back out the door. I called after her, 'Well done! Today, you remembered!' She grinned and said 'Thanks Mom.' "

Treat her as if she already is what you would like her to become: "Well done -- today you remembered!"

This positive thinking can also be applied to sibling fights. Have true expectations that your children can work out their own problems. Children fight for their parents' involvement and attention. Removal or total disinvolvement will sometimes be effective in reducing sibling fights.

The following story reported by a parent who recently completed her second six week T.A.P.P. class demonstrates the success of disinvolvement.

"Andrew age 7 and Jonathan age 10 began arguing at breakfast over who would get to use the coupon on the cereal box to send in to get foreign coins. As I sat down to breakfast the boys focused their bickering on me.

Andrew:
'Jonathan always gets to do things first.'
Jonathan:
'But he always wants things his way.'
Andrew:
'But he already has a bunch of coins.'
Jonathan:
'He had some and lost them.'

I suggested (still using roadblocks) that their uncle was a second source of foreign coins, that I would call him, and that there would be other cereal boxes with coupons to send in later but the whining - at me - continued. Finally, calling on my recent T.A.P.P. skills, I said:

Mom:
'Look this is a problem, one coupon and you both want to use it. I know you can solve it. I'm going in the other room to drink my coffee. You can let me know what you agree on.'
Andrew:
'He won't listen.'
Jonathan:
'He just wants everything his way.'

I left and went into the next room to drink my coffee. They started yelling for me from the other room. I stuck to my guns. I said:

Mom:
'Maybe I'll have to go upstairs and drink my coffee.'

They started discussing the matter between themselves. It was time for me to leave for work and no solution had been found. I announced we had to go. Andrew has wanted to take the pet pigeon to day care with him but the bird was "on loan" to us for the summer from Jonathan's school classroom. Jonathan was reluctant to let Andrew have the bird for a day and Andrew knew it. I sensed yet another argument on its way but said nothing. As I headed for the car I heard:

Jonathan:
'I'll let you take the bird Andrew, if you let me have the coupon.'

Andrew was delighted. Everyone heaved a sigh of relief. As the car trip to daycare began I was preoccupied with time, traffic and a flapping bird in a huge cage beside me in the front seat. Because of the cage, both boys were sitting in the back seat. Their conversation continued.

Jonathan:
'Let's not use Mom to work out our problems any-more. Okay?
Andrew:
(Anxiously) 'But can I talk to Mom if I need ideas?'
Jonathan:
'Oh sure! But we won't use Mom to work out argu-ments, okay?'
Andrew:
'Okay.'

Here Jonathan had proposed working out their problems themselves. Andrew had understood what he was talking about, but feeling overshadowed by his broth-er's negotiating skills, appropriately negotiated for himself to use me, not to solve his problems, but in case he could-n't come up with possible solutions. I just sat quietly tak-ing it all in. I felt an overwhelming sense of reward for a year's worth of work modeling healthy communication."

Ginott, however, offers some ideas for the role of an objective parent referee.

> Protect the safety of the one child without
>   making the other child feel like a bully.
> Encourage the fighters to work out their own
>   solutions.
> Help diminish the rage by encouraging each
>   child to express his hostility toward the
>   other privately -- in pictures, conversation,
>   or writing.
> Make no hateful comparisons.
> Never take sides.
> Give full value to each child's point of view
>   by repeating it aloud.

The same hard working mother tells of her success acting as a parent referee.

"Jonathan and Andrew had gotten along well all day. It was a Saturday and they had spent the entire day in each other's company. Late in the afternoon I had to get ready to go to a friend's house for dinner. I was going to drop the boys off for a visit at their father's house on the way. They knew the plans, and had been instructed to get ready to go. I came downstairs from getting dressed with a few minutes to spare to find Andrew sequestered in the bathroom in tears. Jonathan was in his room obviously very angry. They had been trying to trade micro machines and negotiations had broken down. Immediately when I appeared each began complaining about the other to me and then the name calling started. I asked a few questions to find out each child's "position". I insisted that I was not the person to solve their dilemma, they would have to do that for themselves. I stated each child's problem, expressed confidence (high expectations) that they could solve the problem and left.

'Andrew you're afraid Jonathan is going to force you to make a trade that you feel is unfair. Jonathan you're angry that Andrew won't suggest any trade that seems fair to you. It's a hard negotiation. You will have to solve it yourselves. I know you can. If it's too hard, you could decide not to trade - that's just an idea. I'm going out to the car because we have to leave soon. You come out and let me know how it goes.'

I went to the car and sat for a full ten minutes very worried about what they might be doing to each other. Ten minutes later Jonathan came out in a very good mood. I was amazed. I didn't say anything or ask about what happened. Both boys jumped into the car. Almost as an afterthought Jonathan said:

'We settled it Mom. We decided to give each other back what we had in the first place. We're going to forget this ever happened and we're never going to try this trade again!'

I'm not kidding - those were his exact words. I complimented them on their creative problem solving. My heart was again overwhelmed with gratitude for the positive parenting skills I had learned! "

High expectations can also be constructive when one child hurts another. Children, especially siblings, often fight with each other. They fight over toys, food, games, clothes, territory and the attention of the parent. Sometimes, someone gets hurt. When this happens, the intervention of the parent is usually necessary. To be effective, the parent action needs to instill remorse rather than revenge or resentment. Will a scolding produce remorse? Probably not. A scolding involves shaming, blaming and criticizing. A scolding feels like punishment. Scoldings work best on those children who need them the least, that is, the shy quiet, good child who already feels remorse. On most children a scolding produces feelings of resentment and revenge.

They feel mistreated and misunderstood. They plot to get even. They think the parent action is unfair. They nurture angry feelings against both the parent and the other child.

How can parents intervene effectively and help the hurting child feel better and the attacking child feel true remorse? How can we help restore peace and harmony and feelings of love and acceptance?

Have high expectations that a new approach will work. Maybe we can try to express dismay that someone is hurt without expressing blame or shame.

Last summer two of my grandchildren, ages three and eighteen months, visited with their parents for two weeks. One afternoon we were playing happily with play dough. Theo, the older child, fed the play dough into a "factory" that made long squiggly worms. Cody, the younger child, made play dough cakes and pies and we pretended to eat them. Suddenly Cody wanted to make a long squiggly worm too. Theo waited until her finger was under the lid and smashed the plastic handle of the machine down on her finger. I snatched her hand out and kissed the finger making sure that it was not a serious hurt that needed medical attention. I hugged and held her and talked about her feelings. "You wanted to make a worm with the factory." I paid exclusive attention to Cody until she was quieter. Theo had backed away from the table and was not saying anything. I then took Theo's hand and kissed his fin-

ger too. "You didn't feel like sharing the play dough factory just now." I kissed him again and said "This is the way
people treat people." He came back to the table and kissed
his sister's finger, showing true remorse. Would his reaction to a scolding have been remorse or revenge?

- First:
Give your immediate attention to the hurt
child. Make sure the hurt does not require
medical care. Give the hurt child a hug, a kiss
and a band-aid if necessary. Validate the
hurt with words. "A pinched finger is a serious
thing!" Restate the problem from this child's
point of view. "You wanted to play with the
play dough!"

- Then:
Model a loving response by giving the attacking
child a hug. "This is the way people treat
people." Pick up his finger too and give it a
kiss. Restate what happened from this child's
point of view. "You didn't feel like sharing the
play dough factory!" Above all, resist scolding!

Hope for the best. Have high expectations that
the two children can work it out and let them. Separate
them only if the fighting continues. Save problem solving for another time.

Sharing toys has always created family problems
that need a new solution. **Sharing is not a social skill that
is understood by very young children.** Sharing causes
conflict between the child that has the toy and the child
that wants the toy. High expectations that the "have child"
will eventually share willingly, can ease the situation.

When parents try to force sharing, the conflict intensifies. **Forced sharing creates blame, causes resentment, leads to negative comparison, leaves one child a loser and deprives the kids of the opportunity to solve the problem.** Forced sharing can also lead to a power struggle.

Instead of forced sharing - learn to focus on the feelings of the "have child" while directing your attention and language to the "have not child." Do this in front of both children. Dad says to Jimmy: "Tommy's truck is brand new. He hasn't played with it very much and wants to keep it for himself for awhile. It's hard to share a brand new toy." Have faith that Tommy will play with the truck for awhile and then will let Jimmy have a turn.

Focusing on the feelings of the "have child" will help reduce the conflict and steer the "have" and "have not" toward solving the problem. Expect that they can...expect that they will! A pleasant, up-beat manner can create the kind of family spirit that makes everyone feel good about working together...and, a sense of humor can help prevent a hassle in a deadlocked situation. High expectations will help parents maintain a positive family atmosphere.

TANTRUMS, TIME-OUT AND JEALOUSY

Tantrums:

Screams and temper tantrums come from children who have run out of words. They are full of bad feelings they cannot express. Children, because they are human, are entitled to a full range of feelings -- anger, hatred and jealousy as well as joy, peace and happiness.

Teach your child the "feeling" vocabulary. Share your own bad feelings as well as the good. Learn to listen to words that express anger, hatred, worry and fear. Listen with acceptance -- and without criticism. Remember - children who are able to share bad feelings in words have little need for screams and tantrums.

Time-Out:

Time-out is a calming activity that helps limit a young child's out-of-control behavior. It is useful when both parent and child are extremely upset. Locate your time-out chair in a quiet and boring place.

Use it for behavior that is truly out of control and for children old enough to understand the concept of "wait". (About 2 1/2 to 3 years.)

Tell your child you understand his feeling but his behavior is unacceptable. "I know you're feeling angry and it's O.K., but we can't talk until the screaming stops."

Set a timer for a short period of time that equals the age of the child. (Three minutes for a 3 year old, etc.) Start the timer when the screaming stops - time only quiet time. Tell your child this rule.

Or, tell your *child* to decide when the time out has served its purpose i.e. "When you are feeling calm enough to return, please come back, I'll be waiting. "

Use the time yourself to pause...take a deep breath, and calm down before you resolve the conflict.

Welcome your child back from the time-out chair. "I missed you, I'm glad you're back."

Time-out helps parents and children resolve conflict in a calmer frame of mind.

Jealousy:

Jealousy has been a part of family life since Cain murdered Abel. He thought that God the Father loved Abel best. All children want to feel loved best. They have an unfillable desire for exclusive parental love. This unfulfilled desire is the origin of jealousy - it can never be totally eliminated. It can however, be tempered and discouraged.

Learn to love each child uniquely rather than equally.

Celebrate their differences! Don't ration love or attention for the sake of fairness.

Spend exclusive time with each child.

Give undivided attention to each child.

Learn to accept and listen to strong and dangerous feelings, e.g., envy -- jealousy.

Give no comparisons -- don't shame or blame.

Love each child uniquely rather than equally.

Jealousy -- celebrate their differences! Don't ration love or attention for the sake of fairness.

NATURAL CONSEQUENCES

Many parents are unable or unwilling to let children experience the natural consequences of behavior. The social order of our world can be a successful disciplinarian when children are allowed to learn, first hand, the world's lessons. Too often, however, parents prefer the "rescue but lecture" technique - a method that is not very effective and is certainly not a positive interaction that shows respect for the child. Example:

Sheila repeatedly forgets to take her gym shoes to school on Tuesday, the day for 3rd grade gym class. Mother becomes very impatient with Sheila's forgetfulness, but always drops the gym shoes off at school before the class begins. Every Tuesday afternoon, Mother lectures, scolds, and nags about the shoes - but is unable to let Sheila find out what happens when third graders get to gym class without their gym shoes.

If Mother would allow Sheila to experience the consequences of her behavior, Sheila might change because of the unpleasantness that results in forgetting the shoes.

Not only is the "rescue but lecture" technique ineffective, it also is harmful to the parent-child relationship. The "rescue" eliminates the lesson and the "lecture" produces negative feelings and stops positive feelings.

Allow your child to experience the discomforts of forgetting without interference from you. This process eliminates friction, saves energy and teaches lessons that words can never teach. Parents give up nagging, pleading, scolding, yelling and rescuing. As a result, children give up promising, ignoring, arguing, asking and depending. **A child who always forgets - has a parent who always remembers.**

Children cannot learn to accept responsibility for their actions until they are allowed to experience the natural consequences of their behavior.

PROBLEM SOLVING

Problem Solving is also a skill that depends on the lessons from Chapters One, Two & Three.

Problem Solving was first designed by the Rand Corporation Think Tank to solve the problems of business and industry. It is now widely used in any setting where people are working and living together. When you can't seem to change the way you feel about the misbehavior, and Limit-Choice-Action is not effective over time, the parent's best recourse is Problem Solving.

However, problem solving is not effective in households where parents are still using roadblocks. Furthermore, the parent must be able to understand and state the problem from the child's point of view as well as from their own point of view.

Exercise:

On the following page is a picture that demonstrates that people see things differently. This picture will remind you that you and your child will probably see things differently when the problem belongs to both parent and child. In this picture, many people see an old lady, others see a young girl. Take your time and study the picture until you are able to see both the young girl and the old lady. Problem solving depends on seeing the problem from the other person's point of view.

Success also requires that the parent be ready to give up something, to compromise, as you would if your child were a close adult friend.

Problems get solved faster when we are flexible about "giving away" some pieces or "giving up" some preferences.

Another secret to success is - brainstorm without evaluating. If the parent questions, criticizes or evaluates the child's suggestion in any way, the child (or anyone) will withdraw from the discussion.

Example: If I asked a small committee of adults, charged to raise money for the playground, to brainstorm ideas, and then I criticized the first suggestion offered, would any committee member feel comfortable offering another suggestion? Of course not!

Evaluating your child's suggested solution will work against the success of this very important skill. Instead, **learn to view the child as an equal partner when solving problems that belong to both parent and child.**

Guidelines for problem solving:
Define the problem. Talk about your child's
    feelings and needs.
Talk about your feelings and needs.
Brainstorm solutions and write them down.

Gestalt Figure first published in Puck Magazine, England, November 6, 1915. Credited to W.E. Hill, titled My Wife & My Mother-in-law, now in the public domain.

This gives validity and respect to each idea.
Evaluate each solution. In this step both the
parent and the child have an opportunity to
comment on why a certain idea will or will
not work for them.
Decide which solutions you plan to try. Often
it is a combination of ideas from both parties
that work for both parent and child.
Make a future appointment to re-evaluate....to
see how things are working out.

Some family problems can be resolved as "stand
up" resolutions. That is, they can be tackled quickly and
resolved more or less as they occur. Example:

The kitchen is a mess because your four year old
has been building a fort with the chairs and table.

Mother says:
"I feel worried about tripping over these things. I
don't want to cook dinner when I don't have room to
walk around."
Jack says:
"I feel like I can't build forts anywhere in this old house!"
Mother says:
"You don't have a room to build forts in, and I'm afraid
of tripping over your fort, if it's in the kitchen. Why
don't we try to figure out a solution that will work for
both of us." (Step 1 - Defining the problem.)
Jack says:
"How about a living room fort? There's lots of chairs in
there, and I could make a really big one!"
Mother says:
"Or how about your bedroom?" (Step 2 - Brainstorming.)
Jack says:
"There aren't any chairs!" (Child is evaluating...not yet

trained in problem solving.)

Mother says:

(Pause...Give yourself a minute.....) "There are several folding card table chairs in the hall closet." (The parent is able to give new information because the feelings are now more positive than negative. Be cautious about suggesting too soon and be cautious about adding on a roadblock.)

Jack says:

"Maybe I could use them in my room."

Mother says:

"Well I don't want it in the living room because the family would be tripping over them. **And the kitchen doesn't work for me.** Would you be happy to try the folding chairs in your room? " (Step four - Choosing a solution.)

Mother adds:

"If it doesn't work for you, let me know." (Step five - Making a future date to see if the problem is happily solved.)

Some family problems are best resolved at a time when tempers are cooled, rather than in the heat of the moment of conflict. These are "Sit Down" resolutions, and need a future appointment.

"Sit Down" problems require an act of faith. Parents need to stop thinking of the child as the problem and to have faith in a joint search for solutions.

Step 1.

Respect your child. Talk about the child's feelings and needs: "I know you're hungry when you get home from school!"

Step 2.

Respect yourself. Talk about your feelings and needs: "But I feel frustrated when the food I plan for dinner disappears."

Step 3.

Brainstorm solutions. Accept all ideas, without criticism.

Step 4.

Decide which solutions will work for you and for your child.

Step 5.

Try them out.

The key word is respect. Respect for your child and what he needs. Respect for yourself and what you need. Have faith in the unlimited possibilities of what can happen when two people put their heads together to solve a problem.

The principles of Problem Solving can be used successfully with very young children. Families need to practice solving problems instead of creating them. Successful problem solving involves children in the decision making process.

A 57 year old grandfather, who is a friend of mine, recently accepted the full care of Ben, his 2 1/2 year old grandson for a week. Together they learned to make joint decisions, the value of choices and the satisfaction of solving problems.

At breakfast time, grandfather let Ben choose and fix his own breakfast food. Ben let grandfather pour the milk and juice, but Ben was allowed to choose when it was poured.

At dinner time, grandfather chose to shop for and cook the dinner at home. Ben selected the menu - stir-fried shrimp and vegetable. Grandfather chose a fresh vegetable; Ben wanted a package of frozen, mixed vegetables. Ben separated his vegetables by kind, then ate them in order of preference. Lima beans were new and pretty interesting - carrots were eaten last.

Grandfather and Ben worked together to solve

problems, not create them. They both made choices and participated in decision-making - a skill that can be learned.

In the following practice exercises, play out each role in writing. Write your own "teaching dialogues" using the guidelines for Problem Solving. When creating the role of the parent, be careful to brainstorm without evaluating. Remember, a critical evaluation will feel like a roadblock to your imaginary child.

109

Grandfather and Ben work together to solve problems, not create them.

Exercise 1

My 16 year old has been licensed to drive a car for 6 months. She drives to school during the day light hours and drives frequently on errands for the family within a suburban neighborhood. She wants to use the family car to drive friends to an away basketball game. The game is at night in a small town about 20 miles away from home. The route is simple, north on the freeway about 18 miles. The small town high school is about two miles from the freeway exit.

Role description: You are the father (mother). You are trying to let your children make their own decisions. You are somewhat convinced that authoritarian parental control, especially with teenagers, can cause a tense and hostile family atmosphere. On the other hand, cars and driving are frightening for you. You have always worried a lot about car travel. You do not think your child is experienced enough as a driver to drive at night on a freeway.

You are the 16 year old. You feel experienced as a driver because you've been driving for 6 months. The game will be over by 9:30 or 10:00 p.m. - you will be back in your home neighborhood by about 10:30. You will have friends with you and will not be alone in case of a flat tire or other emergency. You have never had an accident and feel that your driver's training has equipped you with the necessary skills for freeway night driving. After all - you have to start sometime!

_____

_____

_____

_____

_____

_____

_____

_____

_____

_____

Exercise 2

My 4 year old son loves to go with me to the store to buy groceries.When we get there he behaves in a way that prevents me from paying attention to the coupons and the specials and the list I've made of what we need the most, and how much I have to spend. What can I do?

_____

_____

_____

_____

_____

_____

_____

_____

_____

Exercise 3

I work from 8:00 to 5:00, then pick up my children at the daycare center, come home, fix something to eat, put the baby to bed and then collapse. Nancy, my 5 year old, whines and cries and fights about everything.

She won't eat her dinner and won't help with the baby. I'm so tired and she's not making it any easier.

_____

_____

_____

_____

_____

_____

_____

_____

Exercise 4

My 15 year old son is the first one home every day. He's always hungry, raids the refrigerator and eats up the foods I've planned on using for dinners for the rest of the week.

_____

_____

_____

_____

_____

_____

_____

_____

THE NEED FOR INDEPENDENCE

Children have as strong a need for independence and autonomy as they do for food. Somewhere between birth and the age of two, this need collides with the parent's need to control. Temper tantrums, biting, lying, fighting, power struggles even teenage rebellion can be traced to this collision.

Home is the only place kids have to learn and practice independence.

Tight parental controls interfere and will produce difficult behavior problems.

Make sure your limits are legitimate limits, and that your words are not roadblocks designed to control your child's behaviors.

Ask yourself:
1. Do my child's actions interfere with my rights or dignity?
2. Do my child's actions interfere with his health or his safety?

If the answer is "no", let go of control. Stop using roadblocks.

How do we help children become separate, independent people? By allowing them to do things for themselves; by permitting them to wrestle with their own problems; by letting them learn from their own mistakes; by not asking too many questions and by letting children make choices. It gives them a sense of control over their lives.

Don't always have a ready answer. Instead, act as a consultant on decisions that are problems for your child. Help children examine alternatives - help them collect information - but resist solving their problems.

Model - Be flexible - Consult - Accept. Dr. Ginott says, "Share - don't preach. Offer - don't impose. Suggest - rather that demand, and - offer only once - don't be guilty of the hard sell."

MORE PRACTICE...MORE PROGRESS

First,

The Listening:
"You're worried about your grades."
"You're afraid of the dark!"
"You sound angry."
"It's no fun to be alone!"

One secret to success is to only say "You're worried about your grades" and nothing more!   Advice is not absorbed through worry anyway. Advice, when people are feeling bad, stops communication.....it is a subtle roadblock.

Second,

The Language of Description:
Describe what you see.
Describe how you feel.

Telling kids how you feel - "I'm upset," "I'm furious," "I'm mad," "I'm worried" does carry a risk--the kid might say, "So who cares?" If it comes to that, let him know..."I do -- I care about how I feel. And I care about how you feel. And I expect this to be a place where we are all caring about each other's feelings!

Punishment:
What happens when grown-ups punish?
Dr. Ginott points out that punishment leads to feelings of revenge, hatred, defiance, guilt, unworthiness, and self pity. The problem with punishment is , instead of the child feeling sorry, and making amends, he becomes

preoccupied with revenge. In other words, by punishing a child, we actually deprive him of the very important inner process of facing his own misbehavior and suffering a consequence for it.

Limit-Choice-Action:

Children are influenced more effectively by actions than words. It's what parents do....not what they say that counts. Furthermore, parents who take action instead of nagging, lecturing and criticizing, feel better about themselves and about their children.

Set fair but firm limits.

Use choices not threats, and

Do what you say you will do.

"No running through the store! Stay beside me or we'll leave..." "We're going home today. We'll try again tomorrow."

Be sure your choices are acceptable to you - be sure you follow through with action. The success of the process depends on the action. **What you do is far more important than what you say!**

Parents who take action, instead of nagging, lecturing and criticizing, feel better about themselves and their children.

Example: Mother and five year old Teddy are shopping in the supermarket. Teddy refuses to sit in the cart and runs back and forth and up and down the aisles. Mother says, "No running! You might fall or knock somebody else down!" Teddy grabs some cookies and starts to open them. Mother says, "Not now Teddy, it's almost time for dinner!" Teddy takes the cart and pushes it faster and faster away from Mother. Mother says, "Come back here Teddy, I'll push the cart. You go too fast.!" Teddy keeps running and knocks over a stack of soup cans on display. Mother says, "That's it! There'll be no T.V. for you when we get home."

Did the talking halt Teddy's behavior? Why is Mother's last statement a punishment?

Following are some ideas that might have worked out better for Mother and Teddy.

1. Use listening to identify how your child is feeling. "It's boring to shop for groceries."
2. Use a language of description expressing your feelings without attacking character. "But I'm worried about the other shoppers. It's hard to shop when children run in the aisles."
3. State your limit. "No running in the grocery!"
4. Give a choice. "You can walk beside me or ride in the cart or help me find some things on the list, but if you continue to run in the aisles - we *will* go home."
5. Take action. Do what you say you will do!
6. Allow the child to experience the consequence of running in the grocery. The next time you go to the grocery, the child stays home.

The Difference Between Discipline and Punishment:
Limit setting can be as damaging as punishment, or can promote effective self-discipline and parental concern. Positive parents need to be aware of the differences.

Limits that punish are rigid and unchanging.
Limits that cherish are evaluated regularly by
   both parent and child.

Limits that punish are always decisions made
   by the parent alone.
Limits that cherish try to allow children

participation in the process of decision-
making. (When the limits are concerned
with health and safety, participation is not
always possible.)

Limits that punish are accompanied by threats.
Limits that cherish allow feelings but curtail
behavior.

Limits that punish are not connected to the
misbehavior in a sensible way.
Limits that cherish are connected directly to the
misbehavior as a natural, logical, sensible
consequence of that behavior.

Limits that punish are often concerned with
the past.
Limits that cherish with what will happen
now and in the future.

Punishing parents use words like "always"
and "never".
Cherishing parents try to be brief, fair, firm
and friendly, and to involve children in
the decision making process.

*We need to remember
to take care of ourselves and of our own self-esteem
in concrete and tangible ways.*

Feeling Good

TAKE A DEEP BREATH

We have outlined some important elements for successful parenting:

- Parents need training in communication skills.
- Parents need to accept their children unconditionally.
- Children need to participate in decisions that affect their lives.
- And parents and children need to feel good about themselves.

This chapter is designed to help parents handle the stresses of daily living. It is also designed to help parents build self-esteem for themselves.

Dorothy Briggs in her book *Your Child's Self-Esteem - The Key To His Life*, states: **"Self-esteem is the mainspring that slates every person for success or failure as a human being."**

Without self esteem, the positive parenting skills are difficult to apply. Fortunately, the practice , the act, of using effective communication helps parents feel better about themselves, about their children and about the job they are doing. There are times, however, when we need to remember to take care of ourselves and of our own self-esteem in concrete and tangible ways.

Learn to identify and manage the stress situations that occur in your life. Anticipate the times of the day, of the week, or of the month that are difficult for *you.* Build yourself a support system from extended family members, friends from work or friends from your neighborhood or church. You need people to lean on. Strong feelings about stress will lose their intensity when a sympathetic listener accepts them with understanding. Search out a friend who can listen without approval or disapproval...without praise or criticism... and learn to listen to yourself in the same manner. "You can be your own best friend."

The Guidelines Are:

Recognize stress.

Give it a name.

Share it with a friend. - **you can be your own best friend.**

•

Recognize bad feelings.

Give them a name.

Share them with a friend. - **you can be your own best friend.**

Stress and Feelings:

"What are the things that happen to me that make me feel bad?" Share these experiences and feelings with your non-judgmental friend. Remember, anger is a secondary feeling. Try to share your first feelings, the feelings you had before the anger.

Take a deep breath....Pause...Give yourself a minute. Count to ten slowly backwards before you respond to a child's misbehavior. Prepare yourself for a stressful situation.

(10-9-8-7)..."Jimmy, coats belong in the closet, not on the stairway!"

(10-9-8-7)...[Report cards are due this week. I'll try to use listening and catch them doing something right!]

Relaxation Exercises & Calming Activities:

Let your muscles feel heavy, one at a time. Feel every joint and let it go. Work up to your jaw! Finish with your eyes! This is especially helpful when you have trouble sleeping.

Toes
Ankles
Knees
Thighs
Hips
Waist
Elbows
Wrist & Hands
Shoulders
Neck
Jaw
Eyes

Visualization:

Get alone - by yourself - and picture a tranquil and relaxing place. Choose your own favorite quiet place.

"I see a quiet park, green trees, grass and lots of flowers...."

"I see myself alone under the tree."

The following visualization exercise is from *Psycho-Cybernetics* by Maxwell Maltz, M.D., F.I.C.S. He calls this a Do-It-Yourself Tranquilizer.

"One of the most beneficial prescriptions that I have ever given is the advice to learn to return to a quiet center. Build for yourself, in imagination, a quiet, tranquil center, a little mental room. Furnish this room with what-ever is most restful and refreshing to you: perhaps beauti-ful landscapes, if you like paintings; a volume of your favorite verse, if you like poetry. The colors of the walls are your own favorite colors, but should be chosen from the restful hues of blue, light green, light yellow or soft white. The room is plainly and simply furnished; there are no distracting elements. It is very neat and everything is in order. Simplicity, quietness, beauty are the keynotes. It contains your favorite chair. From one small window, you can look out and see a beautiful beach. The waves roll in upon the beach and retreat, but you cannot hear them, for your room is very, very, quiet.

Whenever you have a few spare moments during the day, between appointments, riding the bus or walking, retire into your quiet room. Whenever you feel tension mounting, or begin to feel hurried and harried, retire into your quiet room for a few moments. Just a very few minutes taken from a very busy day in this manner will more than pay for themselves. Say to yourself (and to your children) "I am going to rest a bit in my quiet room." Then, in imagination, see yourself climbing the stairs to your room. Your room is secure. Nothing can touch you here. There is nothing to worry about. There are no decisions to be made here. You left your worries at the bottom of the stairs."

Be specific! Build detail! Use the same place each time you do this exercise.

Take a few minutes - think of your quiet place - write down the description with as much detail as you can imagine. Practice entering this place several times a day until it is easy for you to do. Your quiet room can be an alternative to anger and a calming activity that helps build self-control and self-esteem.

The following exercise is adapted from *Twenty Things You Love to Do*, from *Values Clarification* - by Sydney B. Simon. Learn to do for yourself the things you love to do.

List 20 things you love to do. Big things, little things - it doesn't matter - as long as they are important to you.

Put $ by those things that cost more than $5.00.

Put F and M by those your father or mother did.

Put R by those things that take risk.

Put an A by those things you can do alone.

Put a +5 by those you won't be doing in
      five years.

Put a -5 by those you did not do five years ago.

Circle those you did last week.

Underline the things you have not done for
      a year.

Look at your list as something that tells a great deal about you at this time in your life. Ask yourself what you have learned by considering the following sentence beginnings.

I learned that I........

I remembered.........

I plan to ....

I was surprised that I........

I never knew............

I forgot that I........

Activities That Relieve Stress:

Explore the following activities to find if any of them will help you relieve stress.

1. Release of tension through creativity:
      Writing
      Music
      Painting - Drawing
      Poetry
      Crafts
      Drama
2. Release of tension through physical activity.

Scrub a floor
Clean out a closet
Walk
Run
Play a sport
Work in the yard.

CONSTRUCTIVE SELF-TALK

We all need to learn constructive "self-talk" or "head-talk". When faced with a problem, give yourself a minute of silence before you respond to yourself or to your child.

There are three kinds of self-talk that can help parents deal with children and stress.

Self-talk that identifies stress: e.g.
"I'd better watch it, I'm pretty strung out."

Self-talk that identifies how the child feels:
"He took a short nap - I know he's tired."

Self-talk that rewards with approval:
"Good for me - I stayed out of it - I kept
my mouth shut!"

We are better able to use constructive self-talk if we have learned to think well of ourselves. Use the exercises and skills outlined in this chapter and throughout this book to help build your own self-esteem.

Following are some self-talk practice exercises. Compare a familiar roadblock response to a positive parenting response. Remember to pause, give yourself a minute, before you begin. Think about all of the T.A.P.P. skills we have learned and write an appropriate response. Example:

Problem situation:
Ten year old leaves an open scout knife on the floor of the baby's bedroom.

Destructive response:
"That was stupid. the baby could have cut herself!"

Constructive self-talk:
(Knives scare me to death - being scared always makes me lose my temper - I'd better be careful about what I say.)

Positive response:
"Knives scare me to death when they're close to the baby. I'm terrified he'll cut himself badly and need stitches or worse!"

PRACTICE MAKES PROGRESS

Choose one or a combination of the following skills:
1. Stop using roadblocks.
2. Change the environment.
3. Change yourself and the way you feel about the problem.
4. Listen to feelings - out loud or in your head.
5. Describe what you see and how you feel.
6. Use Limit - Choice - Action.
7. Referee - Restate each child's position.
8. Have High Expectations.
9. Allow Natural Consequences.
10. Problem Solve.
11. Model.
12. Take care of yourself.

Practice constructive self talk and an appropriate response or action from the above list of skills.

Which of the above skills might work for you. (Choose one or a combination of several.) Example:

Kids fighting about which TV program
to watch.
1. - 5. - 6. - 10. - 11.

Problem Situation:

1. Daughter arrives home at 1:30 A.M. after
   promising to be in by midnight.

_____
_____
_____

2. Child is dawdling over getting dressed and
   eating breakfast making Mother late for work.

_____
_____
_____

3. Mother comes in the house and finds the
   living room a mess after she had asked the
   kids to keep it clean for company.

_____
_____
_____

4. Child is disturbing you because he is getting
   the attention of your guests by turning
   somersaults and making funny noises.

_____
_____
_____

Constructive self-talk helps us eliminate the damaging responses we might otherwise make. It reminds us
to be open to learning rather than ruled by our need to

control. It gives us a minute to pause and to think about which skill would help solve rather than increase the problem. It helps us to feel good about ourselves.

*The child's need for independence
is as strong as
the child's need for love.*

*If unsatisfied,
it propels parent and child
into a power-struggle relationship*

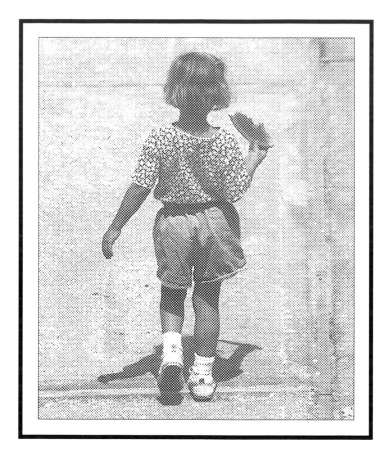

Letting Go

INDEPENDENCE

As described in Chapter Four, children have as strong a need for independence as they do for food. This need surfaces before the age of three. It is a dominant need during the teenage years. It often competes with the parent's need to control. It always competes with the parent's need to protect, and, of course, with time. It is easier and faster to do it for them.

Children, as they grow, need to learn about themselves and their world. These lessons are called "life tasks." The most important life task from two years old on, is to establish independence. Saying "no" is a code saying "I am me - independent from you." (Saying "no" also makes living with toddlers difficult.) Respect for the importance of this life task helps parents stay out of the way. A well established independent personality at two, smoothes the way for the teenage years when, again, the most important life task is establishing an independent personality. It is not always possible for parents to give small children the time and attention that it takes to learn about independence, but when they can , the rewards are worth it. Paula Polk Lillard in her book *Montessori Today* describes an incident that illustrates the advantages of letting even very small children accept responsibility for themselves.

"A mother of a twenty-one-month-old boy said to me recently, 'It's just incredible how much time he takes. It's so hard to get anything done but take care of him. I want to be there for him but it is so frustrating when there are so many things that I want to accomplish.' Then she told me that earlier that day she had been in the yard with her son. He had begun to climb up a five-foot open-rung ladder that was leaning against a tree. After he got to the top, it was extremely hard for him to get down. At first, he tried to turn around and face outward, so that he could see where he was going. He kept trying to figure out how to turn his body around, how to look forward while going down backward. He worked at this for a long time. Finally, he gave up on trying to turn around and began to descend backwards, clutching, with his chubby hands, the ladder rung, dropping one foot down then feeling for the rung below. Eventually, when he found it, he started feeling for the next rung. He was totally absorbed in his activity, concentrating every muscle. Sometimes he missed a rung and hung there, feeling about with his foot. His mother remained next to him, holding her arms out to "spot" for him. Each time he missed, she resisted the temptation to place his foot on the rung. It was hard not to help, but he was so pleased with himself when he managed on his own and gave no indication of wanting help. All the while that he was engaged in this concentrated effort, he was repeating to himself, 'Don't fall, don't fall,' 'Be careful, be careful,' 'Climb down climb down.' When he made it to the bottom after such laborious effort, he said, "Do it again!" and up he went. This process continued for an hour and a half. Then he stopped as suddenly as he had begun. Some inner need was met. He was calm and happy and ready to go inside for his lunch.

After describing this incident to me, the mother said, 'I was so glad that I could take this time for my son that morning.' Of course, it is not always possible for parents to give such help, but it is important that they do so when they can. The rewards are as great to the parent as to the child, both now and in the future when the child grows into a strong and independent adult."

TRUST AND RESPECT

All along the way, involve your children in planning and decision making. Help them explore the world and make it their world. Listen to their ideas. Provide choices from an early age on. Model appropriate problem solving skills. Delegate appropriate responsibilities and trust!

A mother of teenagers said, "How can I trust my daughter when she is not trustworthy?"

Examine the relationship between trust and respect. Trust is a natural extension of respect and loss of trust suggests loss of respect. Trust for the child cannot exist without an atmosphere of mutual respect. Mutual respect is the foundation of a healthy family and the responsibility of the parent *and* the child. Mutual respect will eventually encourage the child to model *your* values and preferences.

MODELING

As we have learned, Problem Solving seldom works when the conflict involves values or personal habits that absolutely do not interfere with the parents' rights or dignity in a concrete and tangible way. Your children are not your possessions. They are human beings, separate from you, and deserve to make their own decisions regarding values, personal habits...and the problems that affect their lives. Learning about climbing down ladders at two, will enhance their abilities to solve the problems and make the right decisions during the teen years.

Take a long view of the choices and value decisions children make during their teen age years. Ultimately, remember that most moral values such as truth and honesty are trans cultural and have been present for as long as mankind has had a recorded history. Your strongest ally for handing down such values is the way you are living your life. **Modeling, rather than lecturing, limit setting or problem solving is the most effective way to hand down values.**

Children are more likely to model your values if your relationship is a good one, devoid of roadblock responses and "good mother" control. Model the behaviors you would like to promote. If Mom and Dad do it, then the child is likely to do it. If you want respect from your child, he must feel respect from you. If you want to teach your child not to hit other children, don't hit your child.

VALUE COLLISIONS

From the beginning, parents and children are caught in value collisions that create family problems. Small children, for example, value noise, confusion and getting up early; their parents value order, quiet and sleeping late. Most teenagers value risk, excitement and irregular hours; parents of teenagers value safety and "a good night's sleep". Family problems flourish. They need to be sorted out and resolved with respect.

The teenagers' fight for independence especially needs to be encouraged. Independence helps them stand against the world for what they believe in and stand against their peers when they want to say "no"....and you *want* them to say "no". They are *best* able to make the right decision if they have been involved in problem solv-

The struggle for independence needs to be encouraged. Independence helps them stand against the world for what they believe in... and stand against their peers when they want to say "No."

ing and decision making from an early age. Again, the accomplishment *felt* by the two year old on the ladder will reap rewards for the parent during the teen age years.

Teenagers often begin this struggle for independence by adopting styles and personal tastes that differ from accepted family practices. The styles change over time, but the struggle for independence remains the same.

In the early 1970's, when I first began teaching parents, pierced ears were a favorite preference for the teenager, but considered inappropriate by the parent. By 1990, the same teenager, a parent of teens now herself, was faced with her girls piercing two holes in one ear and her boys piercing and wearing earrings as well. These practices were as difficult for the '90's parent to accept as pierced ears were for her Mother in the early '70's. It helps to understand that adopting personal choices that differ from family practices is the keynote of the teenagers' struggle for independence....and, when these choices do not interfere with your rights, your dignity or with health and safety, let go.

The following questions are outlined effectively by Thomas Gordon in *Parent Effectiveness Training.* Learn to accept your child's preferences as long as they do not interfere with your rights or needs, or with health and safety. Ask yourself, "Does it cost me anything in time or money? Does it prevent me from going to work or to play? Does it keep me from living my life in the way I have chosen to live it?" If the answers are "no", accept your child's personal tastes with respect. Remember, the teenager's struggle for independence needs to be encouraged, and the respect you give to your child will be returned ten-fold.

Problems That Belong To The Child But Affect The Life Of The Parent

Many problems belong to the child but affect the life of the parent. School troubles, drug and alcohol problems, tough decisions regarding life's choices and even biting, fall into this category. The *Tips from T.A.P.P.* offer the following suggestions to help parents and children through some of these difficult times.

Kids - Drugs - and Alcohol

There are powerful influences at work that affect a teenager's decisions about the use of drugs and alcohol. Sometimes teens feel rewarded by a sense of belonging to the peer group and following their practices rather than to the family. Media messages promoting the benefits of cigarettes and alcohol are another strong influence. The teen years are also a developmental stage that enjoys risk-taking behaviors. Temporarily, these forces can mitigate the influence of sound parenting practices.

Nevertheless we must take a long view and help our children through these years by keeping communication open and making sure we have established a family atmosphere that depends on mutual respect.

How can parents help children get ready to say "no" to drugs and alcohol? Pay careful attention to three well documented observations:

1. Kids who are able to say "no" have high self-esteem -- they think well of themselves.
2. Kids who are able to say "no" understand decision making. They have had participation in decisions that affect their lives.
3. Kids learn social lessons through modeling.

Self-Esteem
- Learn to recognize and listen to feelings.
- Avoid using words that evaluate.
- Give no anxious warnings, threats, lectures or criticisms.
- Encourage.
- Respect.

Decision Making
- Let children make choices.
- Make sure they are a part of decision making that affects the family.
- Resist solving problems for them.
- Give responsibility.
- Ask yourself, "What am I doing for my child that he could be doing for himself.

Modeling
- Model the behavior you would like to promote.

School Problems

There are many reasons why children perform poorly in school. Physical or mental impairment, poor school standards and no time or place for study are some of the obvious reasons. Unrealistic parent expectations, low self-esteem, peer pressure and poor parent-child relationships are less obvious but often important.

Examine each reason carefully - determine whether it is related to your child's school problem - then take the appropriate action.

- Schedule a physical that includes an eye test, an ear test and a test to determine learning disabilities.
- Decide, with your child, on a study schedule

and make space and light available.
- Evaluate school placement and teaching performance. Change what you can (if indicated) and supplement what you cannot.
- Enroll in parent education classes designed to improve communication, change attitudes and build self-esteem.
- And most important, give no anxious warnings, threats, lectures, criticisms or comparisons. The child who has trouble at school, doesn't need more trouble at home.

Biting

"My two year old bites - what can I do? I tried time-out, but it doesn't seem to work. He still bites. My friend told me to bite him back. He cried harder and bit me again the next day. If I spank for biting, he becomes more hostile, and "spanks" me in return. I feel like I'm increasing his rage and his misbehavior and not doing anything to stop the biting."

When handled without shaming, blaming, criticizing or punishing, biting is a temporary way of behaving.

Biting is a sign that the child's living situation is too difficult for him. Frustrated and unable to express himself effectively, he resorts to biting.

He needs, instead, to learn words or take actions that can help him express his feelings. He also needs a simplified environment.

What to do at the moment:
- Listen to his feelings of rage and give them a simple label. "You're very, very angry today!"

"My two year old bites. What can I do?" Simplify his environment -- cut back on play time with others.

- Share your feelings with him in a direct but brief descriptive message. "But biting hurts.......and makes me cry!"
- Make sure he's safe and "vanish" for a little while. "You can play in the playroom, (the fenced yard, the playpen, etc.) I need to be alone right now."

What to do over time:

Simplify his environment by eliminating some of the toys that are too challenging and cutting back on numbers of playmates and playtimes with others. When handled carefully, biting is a temporary way of behaving.

- Do things together that are age-appropriate so that you can run interference when the going gets rough.
- Introduce him to acceptable activities that dispel anger: painting "feeling" pictures, punching pillows or stuffed animals or beating the floor with a rolled up newspaper.
- Most importantly, stop doing the things that are not working such as time-outs, spankings, lectures, shaming, blaming and criticizing. They will only lead to additional power struggles and more unacceptable behavior.

When handled carefully, biting is extremely temporary behavior.

Tough Decisions

Most decisions in life are fuzzy. Rarely is there a completely wrong or completely right choice. Tough decisions can be opportunities to help children learn sound decision making practices. When the parent and the child disagree on the preferred course of action, the problem is best resolved as part of an on-going dialogue designed to avoid a power struggle. That is, the child and the parent need time, in between discussions, to reflect on one another's point of view. The key to successful resolution is respect.

- Define the goals you are both seeking. Search for common goals that you can both accept as well as individual goals that you both may not be able to accept.
- Help your child look at the whole picture. List all of the available options. This step may involve help from outside experts. Listening together to expert advice is a healthy parent-child interaction that shows respect, avoids the power struggle and builds self-esteem.
- Define the problem. That is, listen to and state the issues from your child's point of view and from your point of view.
- Brainstorm solutions. It is critical that no objections or criticisms are raised during this brainstorming.
- Select a course of action that is acceptable to both. If this is not yet possible, let some time go by before trying again, so that each party can reflect once more on the other person's point of view.

THE BOND OF LOVE

In spite of our failures, children remain *very* forgiving and they love us unconditionally until we trespass so much on their individuality that their love becomes diminished and resentment begins to take it's place.

The bond of love between a parent and a child is

strong. Many of the damaging things that parents do or say are forgiven because of this strong bond.

None of us will ever be able to learn a *perfect* language, to *always* listen to feelings, to *never* use a roadblock and to *completely* give up control. But the bond of love we have forged will override our mistakes to a great extent. Nevertheless, our children will grow stronger and happier every time we successfully use a positive parenting skill.

AGAIN - PRACTICE MAKES PROGRESS

The Art of Positive Parenting teaches discipline that works. For many family problems, parents will need a combination of skills. If this seems too complicated or if you are not feeling good enough to make use of every skill we've learned, two thoughts will help you back to the right track. **Stop using punishment and stop using roadblocks.**

Children need discipline....and parents need methods of discipline that work. Punishment is not one of them. Punishment can take many forms. It always involves the use of power and it always damages self-esteem. Screaming, hitting and spanking are common punishments. Verbal assaults that blame, shame and embarrass can be classified as punishment. Grounding and isolation, especially when administered out of the context of the behavior in question, can be forms of punishment.

All of the above encourage rebellion and retaliation, and all are devastating to the child's good feelings about himself and his life situation. All are also included in our list of roadblocks to communication.

People resent punishment. Children are people too. Punishment makes people feel fearful and full of revenge. The fear destroys self-esteem. The revenge destroys acceptable behavior.

Successful family living depends upon mutual respect. Your child cannot feel respect for you until he feels respect from you. **Stop using roadblocks and stop using punishment. They undermine respect.**

The examples that follow show a combination of choices for the parent. What works in one family may not work in another family. What works for you, may be a combination rather than a single skill. Practice using a combination of skills.

Example:
Elizabeth, age eleven, does not get up when her alarm goes off and either misses breakfast or is late for school.

You can:
Stop using roadblocks. Instead tell her how you feel. "I'm worried, frustrated, anxious and angry!" This is a delicate process. Be ready to switch gears and listen to her feelings.

•

Say nothing. Let her continue to be either hungry or late and experience the consequences without interference from you.

•

Problem Solve....Share your feelings and needs and listen to her feelings and needs. Brainstorm possible solutions.

•

Model the behaviors that you value for her. Get up promptly when your alarm rings, eat a good breakfast and be prompt for your appointments.

Practice using appropriate skills in the following examples:

Mary, age five, has crayoned all over her bedroom wall.
You can:

_____

_____

_____

_____

_____

Tommy, age 18, has just come home from his first semester in college. He says," Mom, I'm not going back to school in January. I hated that school. And besides, I don't have any idea what I should be studying."
You can:

_____

_____

_____

_____

_____

Finally, be aware of the forces that work against our ability to use the positive parenting skills. They are:

Time - It is easier and faster to do it for them.

Anger - Learning to handle anger is the work
of a lifetime.

Unfulfilled Dreams - We want them to have
the things we have missed.

The need to be needed.

The need to be in control.

The need to feel important.

The need to protect ..... from failure, from
embarrassment, from harm, from the world.

FINAL COMMENTS

Hopefully, the skills learned in T.A.P.P. will give you a blueprint for keeping your family on a positive course.

Hopefully, the skills will help you develop an accepting attitude, an attitude that respects your child as he is and prizes him as a person, no matter his behavior.

Hopefully, practicing the skills from T.A.P.P. will lead you toward instead of away from the goals introduced in Chapter One.

We want our children to live and to grow----to feel good about themselves, to have high self-esteem----to be self regulated, and to have a high regard for the feelings and rights of others. We want to live in an atmosphere of mutual respect.

And hopefully, the skills will also help you develop a love that views the child as a separate, unique individual, a love that is open to learning and does not possess or control. This is stated so well in these words from *The Prophet* by Kahill Gibran.

"You may give them your love, but not your thoughts,
For they have their own thoughts.
You may house their bodies, but not their souls,
For their souls dwell in the house of tomorrow,
Which you cannot visit, not even in your dreams.

**You may strive to be like them, but seek not
to make them like you.**"

APPENDIX

A Parent's Reflections - A story of one family's experiences before and after their introduction to the skills described in this book through participation in a six week T.A.P.P. class.

"If you'll just forgive me I'll never be bad again," my daughter Molly sobbed. "I promise."

I sighed, something was wrong. I was unable to correct my 4-year old without her dissolving into tears. We both lost sight of the original problem in the scene that followed and we both felt bad afterward. The first time I heard her say those words I felt especially terrible. I was struck with both her desperate need to please and her inability to deal with criticism. This child should feel extremely confident, loved, and secure, I reasoned. She has been showered with attention and love since the moment she arrived!

The fifteenth time I heard those words I had no time for such doubts...or remorse. By that point, I simply felt frustrated and manipulated. And cheated. Cheated of my parental right to nag occasionally and give simple commands that would be followed by obedient responses. Simple things like, "Molly, take your shoes off my glove box. You're making marks on it." or "Molly, I told you, we have to go to the store NOW! I'm sorry that you just got your Barbies out. Let's go!" or "Molly, don't ask me about cake again...one piece is enough!" My requests were endless, I'm sure, but all perfectly justifiable in my mind.

We probably could have gone this way forever had Molly been a different type of child. But it had gotten harder and harder to correct her without hurting her feelings and prompting tears. I was confused. I figured it was important for me to tell her how to behave. After all wouldn't she be spoiled and difficult if I stopped coaching and training her, step-by-step? If I just let her go, wouldn't she just "let go" too? I didn't know and I was not eager to try anything that might take me from a bad situation to an even worse one. Fortunately, for both of us, Molly found a way to let me know

OF POSITIVE PARENTING

that we were traveling a dangerous course.

But let me back up. Molly had always been sensitive and communicative. From the beginning of our verbal relationship she responded agreeably to my rules and suggestions. I was nice to her, and in turn, she was obedient and docile. As she entered her third and fourth years, she remained, for the most part, responsive to my dictates. But, at times, I began to need to rely on bribes, promises, or threats to guarantee her good behavior, particularly in social settings. As long as I was around to remind, prod and reward, I knew I could depend on Molly to be a model child. When I knew we were to be separated, I would recite a long list of reminders and offer a few warnings with my good-bye kiss and, again, she would live up to my expectations. But, there were problems beginning to grow even though I thought I was only planting seeds of good behavior. For one thing, I knew I felt better about her behavior if she were physically near me. If she were within earshot of my view I could guarantee she would behave. People always commented on how obedient and pleasant Molly was which reinforced our pattern. Well it's working I figured. If we can just keep this up till she's 13, we'll all survive and she'll know how to act on her own. But could I keep this up? Could she?

It's no wonder I began to feel tense and strained when anticipating all the interacting she and I would have to do until then. I can only compare it to a tightrope walker who is maintaining his balance but can't see his destination. When Helen (our second daughter) arrived, Molly was 3 1/2. I felt like someone had thrown me a chair to hold while I traversed the tightrope. I can only imagine how Molly felt.

For a while she continued to be well-behaved and "compliant", but less and less easy going. She was happy in certain comfortable settings but not adventuresome or particularly independent. Our verbal exchanges began to change too. When she said to me once, after some slight correction, "I'll be good if you're nicer to me" and I immediately thought, "I'll be nicer to you if you'll just be good", I knew we were going nowhere. The diminished amount of time and attention she was receiving because of the baby contributed to this uncomfortable cycle. I would be very affectionate to her part of the day and remind her that she would "always be my baby" and then when things got hectic, I would urge her to "hurry up", "come NOW", and "please bring me a diaper immediately". I was inconsistent at best. When she began to either cry and whine or belligerently refuse to cooperate, the situation would intensify and end with her sitting on the steps crying. Eventually, she began promising "to do better next time." "Let's just start over", she'd beg. We were both trying for the same unrealistic goal of having a perfect day -- one where we didn't get "off-track". When things would get stressful, we'd both feel as though the whole day was ruined. In addition, I'd feel the extra burden of wondering what I was doing wrong.

One day, though, Molly added a twist to our routine interaction. "I'm going to jump out my window", she yelled as she ran up to slam her bedroom door. My first thought was, "Where did she hear that?" While I didn't really worry that she would actually jump out the window (ironically, she had never even opened one by herself), the intensity and bizarre nature of her impulse frightened me. Whether or not it was an original thought didn't matter; she was feeling bad.

She said similar things on several later occasions, but later outcries of this type seemed more calculated to provoke a reaction from us. Nevertheless, her feeling of wanting to get away from me, to deny me her presence, to hurt me and herself was real every time. At the same time, though, she wanted to shock me enough to make me reach out to her, to reassure her, and to establish contact with her...but on her terms rather than on mine. My overall feeling after about 5 consecutive days of hearing these threats periodically was that if she's feeling that bad, she's hurting and needs something. Ignoring her was out of the question for me. I also figured that at 13 she'd be old enough to open windows -- be they actual windows or other means of escape.

She was running away but basically calling more of our attention to her by doing so.

"What next?" I wondered. I said to several people at that point,

OF POSITIVE PARENTING

"I think we need to see a psychologist...someone who will teach us to say the right things initially so we don't wind up saying the same old lines to each other. If we started out saying the right thing maybe she wouldn't feel that HER self-esteem depended on OUR comments to her about her actions. Also I didn't want to give in to her drama each time and complicate things out of fear of upsetting her. She had begun saying things at this point like, "Mom, you said people are more important than things so why do you care about your dumb lamp getting knocked over more than my feelings". AAR-RGH. When your lamp has just been knocked over you don't need the challenge of explaining that one.

A few days later she came home from the first library story hour saying that she had been good and quiet (unlike "some of the kids, Mom"). Indeed, she had been so quiet that she hadn't participated at all in Ring Around the Rosy ("I might have done it wrong.") or Duck, Duck, Goose ("I might have ended up in the soup."). At that point, I felt like I was the one in the soup. I couldn't imagine how to advise or help her without misleading her. I figured if I encouraged her to quit going to story hour until she felt more comfortable about it ... she would end up a dropout. If I told her to stay and play even if she didn't like it, I was telling her to be a pushover or a follower. And if I told her that I too had been shy in similar circumstances I was reinforcing her shyness based on MY experiences and labeling her as "shy". While I didn't have any answers for her I thought it would help if I tried to focus on what real problem was beneath the surface of the situation. Between her inability to accept criticism or correction at home and her uneasiness in public it was obvious that she was lacking self-confidence. Whatever I said to her, I realized, needed to be supportive and non-judgmental...but what else?

Something in "A Tip from T.A.P.P." caught my attention and intrigued by the emphasis on self-esteem and unconditional love, I called the Crittenton Family Services phone number at the bottom of the article. Seconds later I was talking to Mickey Tobin. I told her briefly of my frustration with Molly's description of her story hour experience. "When a child has a problem, all you can do is listen and make sure she knows that you

understand how she feels.", she said. It sounded so simple, but I felt immediately relieved and inspired. I didn't have to "fix" things for her. I just had
to listen. I felt like I had seen a ray of hope and I signed up for the 6-week
parenting course, The Art of Positive Parenting.

Two days after my call to Crittenton, Molly, Helen and I were headed
to an appointment with Molly's allergist. We had just enough time to park
and walk to the office if we were to be on time. We entered the building
and went to the elevator, but I saw no listing for her doctor on the chart
next to the elevator. Confused, I asked for help at a first floor beauty parlor.
"Oh, he's moved to Cleveland Avenue," they calmly informed me. With my
stomach in a knot and my heart pounding, I asked to use their phone to call
ahead (and their phone book and a chair for Helen...). I called, feeling con-
spicuously out of place at the receptionist's desk. Molly waited patiently by
my side.

A few minutes later we were on the road again and I began nervously
searching for the unfamiliar office building, aware of the minutes slipping
away. At some point I snapped at Molly about something. When we finally
found the office and were parking, I apologized. "I'm sorry", I said, "It's just
that I was worried about getting lost and I was dreading walking in late so I
snapped at you." Out of the blue she answered me, saying, "That's okay
Mom. I understand. That is exactly how I felt at story hour the other day. I
felt so worried that any second the teacher might say 'Don't you wanna join
in honey?' that I just couldn't relax and watch the dumb games."

I smiled and said very little. I had never heard her articulate her
feelings so well, though I had questioned her at length about the whole incident. Suddenly it didn't matter to me whether she ever played the "dumb
games" at story hour. The only thing I wanted her to know was that I recognized that she had had an awful feeling. I felt bad that she had had it. But,
I felt good too because that awful feeling is a part of life and she had dealt
with it in her own way. It didn't matter that it wasn't the way I might have
hoped or that story hour hadn't been as fun as I had envisioned. It didn't
even feel right to preach about being brave and joining in. It just felt good
to listen to her without feeling like I had something to solve. She "owned"

the problem and even though it wasn't a pleasant experience it was hers --
all hers...not mine. She was entitled to have it be her problem and not have
it all tangled up with my doubts, expectations, worries, memories or solutions. Just like having a setback getting to the right doctor's office on time
was my problem. I surely didn't want anyone reminding me at that point
that I could've started out earlier or checked the address before leaving the
house. Worse yet, I wouldn't want someone to dismiss my anxiety as point-
less or to lecture me about "worrying too much". I just wanted someone to
recognize that I was feeling what I said I was feeling.

Intuitively, Molly was doing just that. I began to truly understand
what Mickey had said to me over the phone two days before. Molly made
me see that we were two equal people with two different problems, but similar feelings. The way she had linked the two made me look at Molly in a
new light. Since that morning I have taken the entire positive parenting
course many times. I have read most of the books recommended on the bibliography and I have a hundred other "Molly stories" that reflect the positive
changes in our interaction. We are enjoying each other more with each pass-
ing year. She is more thoughtful, capable and pleased with herself than I
would have dreamed possible when she was four. Several incidents con-
firmed that we were indeed on a new course. For example, soon after that
day, she buckled her seat belt without any prompting from me because, as
she put it, she didn't want to "lose herself". She changed Helen's diaper
from start to finish, which they both thoroughly enjoyed. But perhaps the
most exciting day was when she came home from story hour and I never
asked a thing about it. At 9:30 that night she said, "You know I played all
the games today, even Duck, Duck, Goose!"

The first day of the fall session of story hour a year later, Molly asked
right before going into the auditorium if she could "skip it" if she felt like it
and I said, "Sure." She decided to go anyway and came up glowing with
excitement, having played Simon Says and the Farmer in the Dell. "Mom",
she proudly exclaimed, "I got to be the RAT in Farmer in the Dell!" I never
could have imagined that simply listening to bad feelings could effect so
many positive changes!

BIBLIOGRAPHY

THE ART OF POSITIVE PARENTING

1. Briggs, Dorothy C.; *Your Child's Self-Esteem*;
   New York, N.Y., Doubleday, 1970

2. Chopich, Erika, and Paul, Margaret; *Healing Your Aloneness*;
   New York, N.Y., Doubleday, 1990

3. Coopersmith, Stanley; *The Antecedents Of Self-Esteem*;
   Palo-Alto, California; Consulting Psychologists Press, 1981

4. Dinkmeyer, Don and McKay, Gary; *Raising A Responsible Child*;
   Simon & Schuster, New York, 1973

5. Dreikurs, Rudolf; *Children The Challenge*;
   Hawthorne Books, Inc., New York 1964

6. Dreikurs, Rudolf; *A Parent's Guide To Child Discipline*;
   Hawthorne Books, Inc. 1970

7. Faber, Adele and Mazlish, Elaine; *Liberated Parents, Liberated Children*;
   Grosset and Dunlop; 1975

8. Faber, Adele and Mazlish, Elaine; *How To Talk So Kids Will Listen And Listen So Kids Will Talk*;
   Rawson, Wade Publishers, Inc., New York, 1980

9. Ginott, Haim G.; *Between Parent And Child*;
   The MacMillan Co., 1975

10. Ginott, Haim G.; *Between Parent And Teenager*;
    New York, N.Y., Avon Books, 1969

11. Gordon, Thomas; *Parent Effectiveness Training*;
    New York, Peter H. Wyden, 1970

12. Gordon, Thomas; *P.E.T. In Action*;
    New York, Peter H. Wyden, 1976

13. Harris, Thomas A.; *I'm OK-You're OK*;
    New York, N.Y., Harper & Row, 1969

14. James, Muriel and Jongeward, Dorothy; *Born To Win*;
    Menlo Park, Calif., Addison-Wesley Publishing Co., 1971

15. Kvols-Riedler, Bill and Kathy; *Redirecting Children's Misbehavior*;
    R.D.I.C. Publications; Boulder, Colorado, 1979

16. Lillard, Paula Polk; *Montessori Today*;
    Schocken Books Inc., New York and simultaneously in Canada
    by Random House of Canada Limited, Toronto, 1996

17. Maltz, Maxwell; *Psycho-Cybernetics*;
    Prentice-Hall Inc., 1960

18. Missildine, W. Hugh M.D.; *Your Inner Child Of The Past*;
    New York, N.Y. 10020, Simon & Schuster, 1963

19. Rogers, Carl R. and Stevens, Barry; *Person To Person*;
    New York, N.Y., Simon & Schuster, 1972

20. Satir, Virginia; *Making Contact*;
    Berkeley, CA., Celestial Arts, 1976

21. Simon, Sidney B., Howe, Leland W., Kirchenbaum, Howard; *Values Clarification*;
    New York, N.Y., Hart Publishing Co., 1972

22. Tobin, Mickey; *Handbook For Caring Parents For The Art Of Positive Parenting*; 1980

23. Tobin, Mickey; *Tips From T.A.P.P. Vol. I And Vol. II; For The Art Of Positive Parenting;*
    1989

To Share What You Have Learned.....Give

The ART OF POSITIVE PARENTING
to a:

- Friend
- Parent
- Step-parent
- Adoptive Parent
- Foster Parent
- Grandparent

- Daycare Center
- Nursery School
- Saturday School
- Sunday School
- Church
- Synagogue

Workshop / Seminars can be arranged through T.A.P.P. - P L U S, 61 Jefferson Ave., Columbus, Ohio 43215. Tel. 614-224-TAPP(8277) Fax. 614-224-8279. To register for a six week class in the Columbus area call 614-224-TAPP(8277).

Please send me_____copies of *The ART OF POSITIVE PARENTING* at $19.95 per copy postpaid ($21.43 in Ohio) plus $4.00 per copy for handling.

Please send me _____copies for the bulk rate of 10 books for $150.00 ($158.63 in Ohio) plus $10.00 for handling.

Enclosed is my check for _____

Name_____

Street_____

City_____State_____Zip_____

Send your check or money order with your book order to:

T.A.P.P. & COMPANY, 61 Jefferson Ave., Columbus, Ohio 43215